MW00990325

Courage and Fear

13 April 2008

to: BWHS Students,

Keep your eyes on the Skyline and go for it.

Semper Fi

[signature]

Also by Col. Wesley L. Fox

Marine Rifleman: Forty-Three Years in the Corps

Courage and Fear

A Primer

Col. Wesley L. Fox, USMC (Ret.)
Medal of Honor Recipient

Briar Woods High School
22525 Belmont Ridge Road
Ashburn, VA 20148

Potomac Books, Inc.
Washington, D.C.

Library of Congress Cataloging-in-Publication Data
Fox, Wesley L.
Courage and fear : a primer / Wesley L. Fox. — 1st ed.
p. cm.
Includes index.
ISBN 978-1-59797-119-5 (hardcover : alk. paper)
1. Courage. 2. Fear. 3. Soldiers—United States—Psychology.
I. Title.
BF575.C8F69 2007
179'.6—dc22

                         2007036457

Printed in the United States of America on acid-free paper
that meets the American National Standards Institute Z39-48
Standard.

Potomac Books, Inc.
22841 Quicksilver Drive
Dulles, Virginia 20166

First Edition

10 9 8 7 6 5 4 3 2 1

This book is dedicated to
2nd Lt. Shelton Lee Eakin, USMC,
who was killed in action in Vietnam in 1966.
He was the epitome of the word and meaning of
U.S. Marine in everything that he did.
His untimely death was a great loss to
his family, Corps, and country.

Contents

Acknowledgments

ONCE AGAIN, I HAVE my brother, James, to thank for planting in me the idea and motivation to write this book. He believed that my experiences might help others faced with similar situations. Rather than keep what I learned to myself, he suggested, I should make that knowledge and information available to all who cared to read it. Should others find themselves in a similar situation in the future, they might recall my experiences and possibly gain from following my action or reaction to circumstances.

My wife, Dotti Lu, was again most helpful and supportive throughout this writing period. She both helped with my word usage and gave me the personal time to get the words on paper. I thank Mrs. Rebecca Bier Stevens, my English editor, for making my writing proper and presentable, a task she managed with a nine-month-old daughter demanding most of her time. I give many thanks also to Rick Russell, my editor at Potomac Books, for always being there for me and taking another chance on my work.

Introduction

"THE ONLY THING WE HAVE TO FEAR is fear itself." President Franklin D. Roosevelt stated it well during his first inaugural address in 1933. He continued to define fear as a "nameless, unreasoning, unjustified terror which paralyzes needed efforts to convert retreat into advance." The United States had reached the depths of the Great Depression, and the president was addressing what he called "material things": the stock market crash, the loss of homes and life savings, the lack of jobs, high taxes, and a nonexistent market for farm products.

Following the Japanese air attack on Pearl Harbor eight years later, Roosevelt's words resonated even more strongly with the American people. There was more at stake than "material things," as many Americans expected German and Japanese bombs to fall on their homeland. World War II was under way, and everyone was familiar with that thing called fear. What was going to happen to our world, to our homes, to our way of life, and to us, the American people?

For the most part, we are not effective when our thought processes are affected and influenced by fear. Furthermore, the greater the possible loss to the individual, the more confounding the effects of fear can be. If fear is not handled properly and promptly, it can and will override common sense, good judgment, and a positive decision-making process. Fear affects the emotions and thoughts of everyone at some point in his or her life. While one does not have to be in a combat situation to suffer the most extreme measure of fear—fear for one's life—soldiers in contact with the enemy, as in a firefight, certainly know the feeling.

U.S. Marines have, in a phrase of today, "been there, done that." Contrary to Hollywood's depiction of combat, in my war experiences in Korea and Vietnam, I never saw a Marine paralyzed with fear, unable to get up and move, unable to fire his weapon at the enemy, unable to fight alongside his buddies. If anything, most individual Marines do more than their share in a firefight, and this is a direct reflection of their training and their belief in themselves and the team as well as the cause for which they are fighting. While the Corps has suffered a few individual exceptions to this spirit, which I address in this work, they are isolated incidents, and individuals who do not fight with courage befitting a Marine do not stay in the Corps for long.

I joined the Marines in 1950 at the outbreak of the Korean War. I planned to stay for a four-year enlistment that would include a tour of combat duty in Korea and to return afterward to the farm in Virginia. I was medevaced out of Korea in September 1951 before I was ready to leave my rifle squad in 3rd Platoon, Item Company, 3rd Battalion, 5th Marines, 1st Marine Division. My hope was to return to the 3rd Squad in Korea upon discharge from the Naval Hospital in Bethesda, Maryland, but that did not happen soon enough. I was assigned Military Police duties in the Washington, D.C., area and in spite of requests for duty in Korea, I did not get the assignment until the fighting had ceased.

During these few years, I heard about other Marine Corps duties that I wanted to take on, so I put the farm off for twenty years. Many exciting assignments followed my stint in Korea, including the Vietnam War during which I served as an infantry battalion advisor to the Vietnamese Marine Corps for one year. I extended my Vietnam combat tour of duty for six months and served as the commander of Company A, 1st Battalion, 9th Marine Regiment, 3rd Marine Division. Instead of four or twenty years as a Marine, I lucked out with forty-three; my ranks were private to 1st sergeant and 2nd lieutenant to colonel.

I tell my story in my memoir, *Marine Rifleman: Forty-three Years in the Corps*, which was published by Brassey's, Inc. (now Potomac Books, Inc.), in 2002. During my time in the Marines, I witnessed many examples of others' courage during fearful moments. In the following pages I write about others' fears as well as my own in different situations, how those fears affected them and me, and what we were able to do about them.

While my focus is primarily on my military experience, the thoughts, actions, reactions, and ways of handling fear described in this book apply to situations in civilian life as well. Fear can bombard us in our daily routine; it can leap out unexpectedly in many ways. The more we know about ourselves and how fear affects us, the better we will be able to control our fear and move through it in a positive manner. There is no standard procedures for addressing fearful situations, but we *can* recognize fear, understand the causes of fear, know what feeds fear, and have some good ideas about how to handle fear.

Not all the examples of fear that I provide here are in response to life-threatening circumstances. My purpose is to show the broad area that this emotion covers. In the following chapters I relate two childhood fear situations as well as a wide variety of other experiences, including teaching a class with no training or preparation about how to do so, parachuting mishaps that could well have ended in death, and, of course, combat. I cover my four phases of fear: recognizing fear, identifying its cause, feeding the fear, and handling that fear.

While most of the stressful situations outlined in this work are covered to some degree in my memoir, here I go into more detail and explore the elements of courage and fear that were part of my experiences. In telling my overall story, I left most of my personal thoughts and feelings out of my memoir. The two books, therefore, can be viewed as companion pieces that together tell the whole story.

My love for the Marine Corps and Marines will be obvious to readers of this book. I love reading about what our Marines are doing today in Iraq, way out in front of the force, getting the job done. That is what our country expects of them, and it is in a Marine's nature never to let the American people down.

Why did I have to quit with only forty-three years of the great life? I would yet today love to have a gung-ho Marine on my right and one on my left. Attack! Attack! Attack! And Semper Fi!

1

What Is Fear?

FEAR IS DEFINED IN Merriam-Webster's as "an unpleasant, often strong emotion caused by anticipation or awareness of danger." Some synonyms are dread, fright, alarm, panic, terror, and trepidation, in other words, painful agitation in the presence of or in anticipation of danger. More synonyms are anxiety, cowardice, irresolution, and nervousness. Cowardice! We have many ugly words in our vocabulary, but in my opinion, *coward* heads the list. Fortunately for America, few of our countrymen deserve that title.

The synonyms of fear reminds us that we all, at different points in our lives, experience some form of the emotion. Our world situation, our society, and our way of life, to include some chosen sport activities, can bring us to the threshold of fear. Two examples of fear's universality are my imaginary fears as a child and my mother's fear of thunderstorms.

I enjoyed my childhood in rural Virginia, and I do not remember being confronted with any big fears. As a small child, however, and for some time following, I was afraid of what was under my bed. That was always a dark, mysterious place and far removed from the warm glow of the wood stove in the living room and the laughter of playful family members.

When I was a child we lived in an old farmhouse with no electricity or plumbing, and my mother or father would take my younger brother, Ray, and me to the little upstairs bedroom with a hand-carried coal oil lamp. The lamp did not provide much light and certainly did not illuminate the dark and mysterious place under my bed, where there was plenty of room for the devil and other evil things to hide. I never wasted any time getting in and out of that bed, hoping to reduce the chances of those things grabbing my bare ankles.

While I did not know what was under the bed, I expected the worst. The few times I looked under that bed in the daytime, I could not see anything because it was always very dark. The stories of a relative or perhaps the woman who came to take care of us when my mother had another baby might have planted the fear in my head. Stories were all I needed to take my imagination to a fearful dimension. I fed my fear of the devil and his demons. I was faced with the unknown.

I never really handled, or managed, my childhood fear of evil hiding in the dark under my bed; I eventually grew out of it. Even when I did realize the impossibility of a threat to me coming from under the bed, I continued to get into bed quickly for several more years. A flying leap was still preferable to offering bare ankles.

As a young lady my mother was afraid of thunderstorms. If one were building up with heavy black clouds and threatening while my father was at work, she would place her four babies, from one to five years old, in our car and race to her mother's house, miles away. I never knew the cause of my mother's fear of storms; she never talked about it to her children.

She didn't appear to be bothered by storms in later life.

She learned to handle her fear or at least kept her feelings within. Her fear is further evidence that we all are subject at different times to dread, alarm, anxiety, and nervousness, the synonyms of fear. I, and I suppose my mother, grew out of our fears, and in a sense this is handling fear.

My mother's fear of storms is an example also that one's fear is not necessarily passed on to others. In spite of my mother's reaction to thunderstorms in my youth, her dread or fear never passed on to me. I enjoyed storms; I viewed them as justification for taking a break from outside work. When a storm came up while I was working in the fields, I would drive my team of horses to a huge hickory tree for shelter and take pleasure in watching the storm under the protection of the tree. Yes, I knew that lightning struck trees, but I never had a fear of lightning striking me. There were plenty of other trees on the farm to share the lighting strikes. During these times, I felt a closeness with God and nature and I relaxed.

I am in full agreement with President Roosevelt's statement, "We have nothing to fear but fear itself." In addition to fear bringing on stress, anxiety, and actual sickness, it can also cause us to perform or fail to perform actions that, in turn, result in personal loss or permanent psychological damage. Fear can cause irrevocable harm to one's personality. Someone who succumbs to fear will never be the same man, not in the eyes of his friends, in the eyes of those who know him, and—most tragic—in his own eyes. Fear can ruin a person. On the positive side, fear, if handled promptly and correctly, causes us to recognize what needs to be done and to get on with the solution.

I rate the Marines at the very top of humanity for the way they handle fear. When it comes to doing the undesirable, they are the best for the job. Many times, I have heard a Marine say, "The difficult we do immediately; the impossible takes a little longer." What a beautiful expression of mental constitution and preparedness! Where does the Corps find this resolute individual, this young warrior?

First off, the Marine Corps attracts a certain breed of applicants. The young people who want to be Marines want a challenge, and they want to be with the organization they feel is the best. For the most part, the Marine wannabe's mark is higher on the achievement pole than the average person's, and he feels that he has what it takes to reach that mark. The Marine Corps ensures quality within its ranks by weeding out those applicants who will not make it. As Marine leaders say, "Old breed or new breed, it doesn't matter as long as he is the Marine breed!"

The Marine Corps screens for the Marine breed at their Officer Candidate School in Quantico, Virginia, and two boot camps at Parris Island, South Carolina, and San Diego, California. I believe that the Lord made us all differently. Each of us has something that we can offer for the good of humanity and our society. Some are good with their hands, some are gifted with language, and others have great minds and brain power. Not all humans are made to be Marines; many can (and should) contribute to the welfare of our nation in other ways. The primary purpose of Officer Candidate School and boot camp is to weed out those who cannot handle heavy mental and physical stress. This is not an easy task. A few get by the screening process, but for the most part, only those capable of taking on the impossible tasks join the ranks of Marines.

Candidates and recruits who cannot handle fear in the manner required (by functioning mentally and physically under stress) are not only a danger to themselves but can also cause the loss of others' lives. I would hope that those individuals depicted in the Hollywood movies who are unable to do anything while under heavy fire are those who are weeded out in the Corps' initial training and evaluation process.

If a person cannot function in a situation similar to the actions on the beaches of Iwo Jima in World War II or the Chosin Reservoir of the Korean War or the A Shau Valley in the Vietnam War, he is no good to the force. He is no help to the team effort, and he may well cause many others to pay the supreme price. This is especially true if he is in a leadership position. A Marine leader must be able to think in the face of grave danger, make the correct decisions about the best use of his force, and move out. Marine leaders move out in front of their force and yell, "Follow me!"

However, even in the Marines, a few (a very few) get by the screening system. In the following sections I will share three examples of individuals whose personal fear interfered with their Marine Corps duty in the Vietnam War.

When I was commander of Alpha Company, 1st Battalion, 9th Marine Regiment, 3rd Marine Division, I had a 1st sergeant who was afraid to spend a night in the bush with our company. He was good with his administrative duties and handled the paperwork at our secured rear base in a suitable, timely fashion.

Alpha Company was always in the bush, running a company patrol base, on patrol, on an operation, or performing any of the other actions that involve Marine rifle companies in combat. I had Marines coming and going into and out of the company constantly. These included our combat casualties, Marines on Rest and Recreation (R & R), Marines going home after completing their tours of duty, and new Marines reporting in as replacements. Someone had to be in the rear at the Quang Tri Marine Corps Base to handle this personnel situation and the 1st sergeant was my man.

But there was a problem: he was afraid of the bush.

He did all of my paperwork back in his tent, as was the normal routine for the other rifle companies. Some of that paperwork required my signature, and to get that, the 1st sergeant had to bring the papers out to me. He came out to the bush for my signature only when he could be assured that a helicopter would be at my position to return him safely to home base later the same day. When there was limited helicopter support or the possibility of bad weather, he did not come out. He was honest about it; he did not hide the reason he would not come out. He told me of his fear, especially at night, and I accepted it as he was doing a good job for me otherwise. The company and I gained more from him in the rear than on the operations with us.

One day bad weather came sooner than expected, and the 1st sergeant was stuck out there with us. He did not stay in my company command post (CP) but chose to spend the night with the 2nd Platoon sergeant. There was no enemy activity that night, but many Marines in the 2nd Platoon did not get much rest.

Sgt. David A. Beyerlein, the platoon sergeant, came to me the next day with a strong request that the 1st sergeant never be allowed to spend another night in his command post. The 1st sergeant had not closed his eyes all night and instead spent the time "seeing" enemy soldiers walking out there in the dark. He had wanted to throw grenades and fire his pistol at them, which of course would have been a danger to the Marines on the defensive line forward of the platoon command post.

Sergeant Beyerlein had spent the night restraining the 1st sergeant and trying to convince him that there were no enemy soldiers forward of their position. The 1st sergeant could not rationalize his fear, break it down, lay it out, and see it for what it was. He was concerned for himself, only.

Delta Company had a worse case of concern of self or cowardice, and for this individual, it was a career killer (and, I imagine, an ego shatterer). This gunnery sergeant was a drill instructor with me in my company at San Diego in 1956. We never worked together, but I knew him well enough and was never impressed with his personality. He was arrogant and boastful, but even so, I never saw in him what he turned out to be.

Delta Company had experienced a small firefight, which cost them a few casualties, both dead and wounded. A chopper came in for the casualties, and the gunnery sergeant, unhurt, placed himself on the medevac bird while casualties were being loaded. On his own, he was departing the area. He had had enough! He could lose his life in this place; the Marines at his feet were evidence of that fact.

The company commander, Capt. Edward Riley, was on the scene and made the gunnery sergeant get off the helicopter. They were short of Marines and the gunnery sergeant was needed. He got off the UH-1E helicopter and stood to the side. The chopper revved up its engine and blades for departure, and just as it started to lift off the ground, the gunnery sergeant ran, jumped on the skid, and pulled himself up into the cabin with the dead and wounded Marines. He was gone. He was out of this Marine infantry mess.

Captain Riley did not want him after that action, even if, by chance, he returned to the rifle company. Because I was out in the bush, as we all were, I never heard what happened to this bum, but I know Ed Riley made sure that his time in the Marine uniform was over. Knowing the Marine Corps and its leadership's expectations of Marine conduct, as well as his duty performance, I would wager that this man had plenty of time to regret his decision and action. His flight from the battlefield surely fit the definition of that ugly word, *coward*.

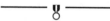

Three 2nd lieutenants, fresh from the Basic School at Quantico, Virginia joined Alpha Company in late December 1968. Like all young Marine leaders, their hope was to receive command of a Marine rifle platoon. I needed them, as I was losing several lieutenants who had completed their time in the bush. Two of these young men impressed me during my initial interview, and I gave them rifle platoons.

The third, whom I will call Rutland, did not impress me as someone who would motivate and inspire others. True, this was a snap judgment based on how he presented himself during my interview with him. However, I noted several characteristics that were not in his favor: He talked too much, and what he said, for the most part, was not relevant to my questions. His mouth ran constantly, and he never looked me in the eye while talking to me. I had several weeks yet before I needed another rifle platoon leader so I assigned Rutland as the Weapons Platoon leader.

The company's machine guns were always attached to the rifle platoons, leaving only the mortar section actively in the Weapons Platoon. Staff Sergeant Willie J. Talley was the Weapons Platoon sergeant, and he did not need a lieutenant as he had the mortar section in the palm of his hand. (Talley was a real Lou Diamond, one of the Corps' greatest mortar Marines of World War II fame.) Talley's leadership allowed us time to observe and know more about Rutland before placing him where other's lives and well-being depended on his ability to make the proper decisions.

Several weeks after our interview, I, again, was not favorably impressed with Rutland. We were in a secure position and my mortar Marines had built a nice bonfire after dark. On my rounds through Alpha's area, I heard them talking and moved closer. Upon hearing Rutland's voice, I paused to listen.

My Marines were bragging about their high school days—girls, cars, booze, the works. No matter what any Marine offered from those good old days, Rutland had to beat it. He had enjoyed relationships with more women, his automobiles were hotter and faster, and he could really put away the booze. This one-upmanship fit with my earlier evaluation of this individual's abilities as a leader. He was not interested in learning about his Marines and what was going on in their minds; he was too busy trying to impress them with who and what he was.

I could not use my mortars on my company patrol mission on February 22, 1969, because the jungle in the area was so dense, I left them and Rutland on the ridge with the battalion. After losing my rifle platoon leaders in our fight that day, Rutland was the only officer I had left. The next day, I gave him a rifle platoon. (Several lieutenants who had done their bush time with Alpha Company earlier volunteered to come out as replacements, so I was shortly in good shape officer wise.)

About ten days later, one of my squads on patrol detected an enemy ambush covering a trail. The enemy was unaware of the squad's presence as the Marines were moving quietly in the jungle about 100 yards off the trail. The squad leader's point rifleman saw a North Vietnamese soldier stand up from his machine-gun position and stretch. The rifleman signaled for the squad leader to come forward; the squad leader decided to assault that enemy position. All enemy soldiers were killed and one Marine was wounded.

Sometime later in the day, the squad leader reported that he had inadvertently left the wounded Marine's rifle at the ambush site. I told Rutland to send a squad from his platoon down to recover the rifle. As a plus on the leadership side, Rutland elected to go along with the squad, which is an excellent way to learn about a subordinate leader's technical and tactical proficiency—provided the senior leader accompanies only with his eyes and ears. (Unless asked, he keeps his mouth shut and his opinions to himself. He can, of course, provide a critique of the squad leader and squad's performance later.)

On this occasion, the squad leader, a lance corporal, moved down the trail, rather than staying parallel with it in the brush, as the earlier squad leader had done. The weapons recovery squad was ambushed on the trail short of its objective, and the opening volley of the attack cut down the first three Marines. Rutland was instantly on the radio, begging me to bring the company down to save him. He would not release the radio talk button so that I could respond to him. He just kept begging me to save him, telling me that the enemy was really tearing them up. I sent the lance corporal and squad that had been out that morning as the reaction force, and that ended that. The experience also terminated Rutland's time in a Marine uniform.

A pessimistic attitude or outlook affects an individual even more than usual when fear is among his or her emotions.

Delta Company's gunnery sergeant surely must have been of the pessimistic variety. Of all the Marines in the company, he alone could not take it. The company was not in contact, there was no fighting or shooting taking place, and the threat had been stable for several days. As had the 1st sergeant and 2nd lieutenant, he assumed that the worst was going to happen to him. Thankfully, there was no negative influence on Marines associated with these three individuals of which I was aware. That lack of influence on others probably was because of the limited involvement of any of the three in our major firefights.

Fear with its many synonyms can encompass a broad range of emotions, as I have presented here, and all of us at times are confronted with different types of fear. The more we know about a particular fear and how it affects us personally, the better chance we have to recover and leave it behind us.

2

What Is Courage?

THE WORD *COURAGE* MEANS having the mental or moral strength to venture, persevere, and withstand danger, fear, or difficulty. Courage also implies firmness of mind and will in the face of danger or extreme difficulty. Synonyms include mettle, spirit, resolution, and tenacity. I particularly like the word *tenacity*, which implies stubborn persistence and unwillingness to admit defeat. I have known many Americans who exemplify tenacity. They are the source of my motivation to write this book.

Courage is part of our daily lives and our many uses of the word demonstrate our understanding of its meaning: "He has the courage of his convictions" or "She has the courage to do the harder right over the easier wrong." We recognize that sometimes "It takes courage to tell the truth," and courage is implied in the statement, "He stands up for his beliefs." His beliefs might not be popular at the time and standing up for those beliefs might cause embarrassment. But individuals with courage do not seek the easy way out or go with the flow if that response or action does not fit with their beliefs.

Where does one acquire courage? Can it be learned? If so, does learning to be courageous involve a classroom? Is there an educational institution anywhere that offers a degree certificate in something so important to us as individuals and to our society? The level of courage an individual demonstrates in any given situation is determined by the nature of the individual, and the development of courage starts in childhood. Our parents move us in the proper direction, and leaders we encounter during our lives help us become who we want to be by setting good examples. Knowing about courageous individuals, learning about their ordeals and how they handled them, can help us attain this great and necessary trait.

I believe that courage is the most important of our character traits. Without it, we tend to fall short in other areas. Without courage, we may take the easier way out; we may lie, cheat, or steal if faced with certain dilemmas in our lives. There is no greater personality trait than integrity, but without the courage to hold fast to our beliefs and to be the person that we want to be, our integrity slips away.

One's outlook on his or her life can influence how courageous he or she is. People with an optimistic outlook tend to be more courageous when faced with undesirable events and happenings. Since they believe that "Everything happens for the best" or "I will come out of this OK," these individuals never envision themselves taking the big loss, going down for the final count, or paying the supreme price.

Pessimists, in contrast, do not usually believe that they will come out of a bad situation satisfactorily. Because of this, pessimists who perform courageously deserve the fullest recognition for their performance. Difficult situations, especially those that could cost one his or her life, are hard to face for all of us. Nevertheless, the person with the negative attitude will have a harder time accomplishing difficult tasks.

Most people perform and exhibit reactions to dangerous situations as a pessimist or an optimist as discussed above.

However, I feel that many of us to some degree move along a continuum of pessimism/optimism given certain events. Happenings in our daily lives tend to swing us between the two outlooks and manners of reasoning. We are also influenced by other people's expressed opinions, what is happening to those around us, and what has happened to those we know well and love.

I am an optimist. In my Marine role, if I ever gave an issue serious consideration, I was comfortable with the thought that I would not go down for the long count. I might be tagged or wounded in combat, or whatever, but death was not a part of my equation. I experienced the deaths of Marines and corpsmen in my units, members of the team, in both wars. Although I was afraid at times, I never came face to face with the thought that I would be killed. I came close but, again, individual optimism is what helps Marines do the impossible when it has to be done; it is what makes the U.S. Marine Corps what it is today.

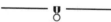

Once, however, my optimistic attitude did not work for me. Because of the needs of the Marine Corps during the Vietnam War, my best friend and I were temporarily commissioned to the rank of 2nd lieutenant along with many other Marine staff noncommissioned officers. At the time, GySgt Shelton Lee Eakin was stationed at the 8th and I Street Barracks, Washington, D.C., our showboat of the Corps, and I was assigned with Supreme Headquarters Allied Powers, Europe, in Paris, France. We received no officer training and, of course, were commissioned out of our current gunnery sergeant billets. My family and I returned to the States. I planned to visit Shelton and his family in Washington, D.C., as we were headed for the Vietnam War shortly.

That visit did not happen. Waiting for me at my mother's home was a letter from a mutual friend informing me of Eakin's death in Vietnam. I have never been so shocked or shaken by anything. I could not believe what I was reading. How did he get there so fast? How and why was he killed so soon in combat? Shelton Eakin was one of the best Marines I knew; he could do anything, and he did it all with Marine perfection, the Marine Corps way. Because I knew his capabilities and his military worth, I had placed Eakin with me in that hands-off position. Like me, he would never die fighting with the Marines. He might go down, but not for the long count.

Eakin's death left me empty, lost, and I began to think pessimistically. I realized that if a bullet had Eakin's name on it, one could well have mine on it. It took me a long time to get over my loss—my loss of faith as well as the loss of a friend and Marine. Fortunately, I had a year to work it out before my orders came through for Vietnam.

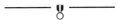

In my initial Marine Corps training, the Corps did not have programs or classroom sessions in which courage was taught directly; nevertheless, the trait was covered in other ways. To be sure, the word *courage* was used and we became familiar with its meaning, but we developed an understanding of the importance of courage to the individual and his unit mainly by being involved with each other, being a member of the team, and training in general. We trained in fire team and squad maneuvers, and we became comfortable and proficient in firing all weapons. Courage, naturally followed tactical and technical proficiency and being prepared to do what had to be done. Awareness of Marine Corps history was also a part of our foundation in courage, but not to the degree that history is used for that purpose in the Corps today.

Currently, those undergoing evaluation and training to become Marines get a bigger slice of the courage apple. While training is designed to build strength and endurance progressively, recruits are also taught "Corps values" in over twenty hours of instruction in courage and commitment. Today's recruits are given reading assignments on individual Marine actions, and drill instructors relate stories of what Marines have done on the battlefield in past wars.

Recruits learn about Marines' involvement in seemingly "no win" combat situations, which the Marines overcame because of their tenacity and determination. Real attention-getters are the severely wounded Marines who stuffed amputated limbs, arms and legs, into the dirt to stop the blood flow so that they could continue to fight off the enemy. These courageous acts have raised the bar of individual achievement and act as a goal and a guide for those who follow. Therein lies the secret of what makes a U.S. Marine so proficient on the battlefield.

———— ♻ ————

Being a member of a proficient, capable team fosters courage. "Together, we can do this thing!" Knowing that your team members will always be there for you inspires the courage to hang on and do what has to be done. Further, no Marine wants to face the other members of his team tomorrow knowing that he fell short today, that he did not do his part in the fight, that he left the fight to his buddies. We all do our part in these situations; we have to.

Here, I am reminded of a negative Korean War experience. During our assault north in the spring of 1951, my squad recovered an Army soldier who had been captured earlier by the Chinese. His story to us, including how he happened to be free and living off the land, was quite long, and I will not go into it here. However, the relevant details of his experience are as follows:

He was fresh over from the States and assigned to a rifle squad. When the Chinese hit the squad on his first night in the line, he realized that he was alone. His squad and platoon members had left their fighting positions without telling him—they "bugged out" on him. His fellow soldiers (individually, I assume) simply faded away in the dark of night. The soldier was forced to surrender when the Chinese entered his position.

The soldier's squad was lacking courage. No one is going to do well on a team that operates as every man for himself, a rifle squad of one. Few individuals would muster courage of any level if they could not depend on the people on their flanks. Marines of my squad never bugged out on their buddies because they each wanted to help and protect one another. They felt courage fueled by pride and obligation.

Adventure is a concept that involves both courage and fear. The word suggests excitement, fun, and experience of new and different things. The desire for adventure is one of the main attractions of the Corps to those young men and women joining the ranks of Marines. And if adventure is experiencing something new, that does not come easily, and that some people cannot handle, then Marine Corps boot camp fits the bill. A Marine drill instructor does his part to ensure that the recruit has no dull moments; the recruit's time is filled with moments of fear and displays of courage.

I am reminded of my Marine Corps recruiting tour of duty from 1957 to 1960. Young men would visit the four armed-service recruiters, all located together in the large second-floor balcony of the post office in Alexandria, Virginia, to learn what trade or skill they might expect to learn in each service. The other three recruiters responded to the question "What do you have to offer me?" with long lists of schools and opportunities to learn a trade; their focus was on what skill one could personally expect to obtain from joining their service.

My response to that question was simply, "If you make it through boot camp, you'll be a Marine!" The majority of the potential recruits would depart with laughter and smart remarks. However, my answer took root in the few who desired adventure and challenge and who wanted to be measured with the best in the warrior business. I always easily made my recruiting quota, and none of my recruits were rejected from Parris Island.

Adventure offers opportunities for individuals to act courageously, to be involved with others in courageous endeavors, and, probably most important, to recognize that he or she possesses courage. We like and seek adventure because it allows us to have experiences we have read and dreamed about.

Fear is a part of adventure, and learning to overcome fear is one of the benefits of embracing adventure. Many people rank adventure based on the danger to the individual participant; the higher the risk factor, especially risk to life, the higher the adventure is rated. Would leaping a motorcycle over several parked cars be an adventure or a foolhardy stunt? Is jumping out of a perfectly good airplane with a parachute on your back an adventure or a death-defying act?

Individual courage is required to handle the fear raised by these high-risk adventures. And I suppose the requirement of individual courage is a major enticement to those who seek adventure. Young men and women joining the U.S. Marine Corps know that fearful moments await them. They feel that they have the courage to overcome difficulty, unless they have been kidding themselves all along about who they really are. The few who have overestimated themselves will drop out along the way. Those who become Marines continue on and enjoy the realization that their courage measured up. They handled fear and continue to seek adventure.

—————— ⚕ ——————

Courage comes in many packages and exercising the trait is not exclusive to those in uniform. Those covering the home front are equally courageous, if not more so. My wife, Dotti Lu, is a great example. We are in love, very close, and always involved with each other's wants, needs, and daily lives. She has always supported my desire to serve the Marine Corps, wherever and under all circumstances. I wore the Marine uniform, but she is every bit as much a Marine as I am. If there is really an eagle, globe, and anchor-shaped heart within the chest of Marines, her heart is shaped likewise.

A fifteen-month unaccompanied Pathfinder tour of duty on Okinawa caught us (we knew it was coming) three months into our married life. Six years later, I was sent to Vietnam when she was eight months pregnant with our second child. Because the birth was so close, I seriously considered asking Headquarters Marine Corps for a delay in my deployment, as I wanted to be with her for the birth. My wife, however, handled the situation like a Marine.

Dotti Lu knew that I believed a Marine's duty is to fight his country's battles and that I was pleased to receive the orders. She also knew that I felt a strong desire to be in both places. As we talked over my plan to ask for a modification to my orders, she responded, "You cannot help with the birth, and the sooner you leave, the sooner you will return to us." While she was extremely concerned about the danger I would face going to war, she courageously accepted her duty as a Marine's wife. Dotti Lu recognized and shared my feelings of a Marine's duty to his country. She understood that "When the bugle blows, I have to go!"

As if that were not a heavy enough burden to place on the one you love, I compounded the problem six months later. When we met in Hawaii for my Rest and Recreation leave, I had a big request of her. I was dissatisfied with my tour of duty as an advisor with the Vietnamese Marine Corps (the situation is covered in detail in my memoir), and therefore, I wanted to extend my twelve-month combat tour of duty for six months and serve with our Marines in the north.

Dotti Lu accepted my reasoning for wanting the additional service and hesitantly agreed through tears. "If you really feel that you have to, I support you. I can get through another six months." I later learned what I had asked of my wife and what she gave to me.

Amy, our second child, born three weeks after I left for Vietnam, was a colicky baby who allowed my wife little sleep, night after night. But what really wore on Dotti Lu was the constant, daily worry that a uniformed Marine would ring her doorbell with bad news from Vietnam. When she agreed to my request, she accepted another 180 days—4,320 more hours—of dreading that uniform at her door. Courage does not come in stronger packages.

For the Marine in combat with a rifle company, not every moment involves a firefight, incoming artillery, or mortar fire; his life is not constantly under threat. He sometimes has days in which he enjoys life with no threat of any kind. The same is not true for the wife and mother at home, who have no way of knowing when the Marine is facing activity that could take him away from them. The dread of that knock on the door consumes every moment. Courage is required for those both in uniform and out.

Courage Handles Fear

A HUMAN BEING'S REACTION to fear can be studied and grouped into four parts: recognition, cause, feeding, and handling. In this chapter I explore these different phases. Understanding how fear works can help you handle, and ultimately defeat, your fear.

Recognition of Fear

Recognition of a threat to one's well-being can come in many forms, and affect us in different ways; the same person can react differently to fear even in similar situations at separate times. During my fearful moments, I am sure I had physical symptoms, such as a pounding heart, rapid breathing, and heavy sweating, but while involved in action, I was not aware of any of this. If I were not physically active, fear usually created a sick feeling in the pit of my stomach and a feeling that I had more on my mind than I wanted to handle, something like a major headache.

Time can appear to stand still or race ahead for us during fearful situations; a few seconds can seem like forever. During a Chinese night attack against my squad in the Korean War, the enemy had overrun some of our fighting positions; they were behind and all around me. I had to get out of my hole and join my squad members to my right. In order to clear the enemy soldiers away from my position for my exit, I activated a grenade and lay it outside my fighting hole. I planned to spring out immediately following the grenade explosion. But, distracted by fear, I forgot to count, and after waiting for what seemed like forever, I decided the grenade was a dud. Still, I had to leave the hole. Fortunately, the grenade exploded just before I lunged up and out.

Similarly, during my first parachute jump I forgot to measure time and a few seconds seemed to last forever. A parachutist expects his parachute to open at the end of a count to four. During my first jump, I forgot to start my count, and I waited for several long moments in fear that my chute would not open. I was relieved when it finally did.

When one is not aware of an immediate threat to his life, naturally, he experiences little to no fear. Here I feel it appropriate to mention two times I nearly lost my life. My first unknown close call was on June 8, 1951, in the Korean War, when six machine-gun bullets passed through my blanket roll and pack on my back as I lay on the ground firing at an enemy machine-gun position. One round, through my entrenching tool handle (the tool was attached to my backpack with the handle laying on my buttocks), did get my attention with an explosive sound and the smart spanking of my butt. I was at a loss as to what hurt me until later when I was asked, "What happened to your pack?" I was not aware (because of my action and the combat noise) that the machine gunner had gotten that close to me.

The other close call came during a free-fall sport parachute jump in October 1964, when a jumper over me (Rick Valley) fell through my opening parachute. Valley's boot caught my canopy as it opened, ripping out an entire gore. I felt the chute open violently, differently from the normal opening, but I was not aware of the reason. Seeing the shape of my canopy left no doubt that I had to deploy my reserve, which I did without incident and with little stress. Only on the ground later did I learn that Valley fell above me and almost hit me during my canopy deployment. This was another close call with death but absent of fear because of the unknown.

Identifying Causes of Fear

In general, an individual feels fear when circumstances create expectations and/or demands beyond normal experience or routine. More specifically, fear is caused by the following: a desire not to suffer loss; involvement with the unknown; placement in a difficult situation; receipt of little or no support from others in the situation; and lack of familiarity with, preparedness for, or qualification for a situation.

When the cause of fear is a threat against the life of an individual, fear's effects are multiplied. Death is our greatest worry, and rightly so; after all, we have but one life to give for any cause.

The causes of fear are as many and as varied as fear itself. And, in some cases we are responsible for bringing fear upon ourselves, although this realization may not help us handle the fear any better. Knowing the cause of a fear can help in handling it as well as give us a chance to keep it from approaching us. If we know we cannot handle a certain situation without undue stress, we may be able to avoid it, to move on, and/or to take a different route to our objective.

Feeding Fear

Next, we look at some ways our fears are fed and situations that can cause our fears to grow. The length of time that we experience a specific fear depends on the situation we are in. If we recognize the cause and do something about it, the fear may diminish or even go away. But if we feed fear, it can get unbearably worse. Fear can be fed by a variety of things: negative personal thoughts about the situation at hand; the negatively expressed opinions of others involved; too much time to dwell on the situation; poor performance by oneself and/or others; a lack of support and authority; exhaustion; and a lack of faith in the cause, organization, and/or leaders.

An experience I had in the Korean War is a good example of how poor performance by others can feed one's fear. On May 19, 1951, as my battalion moved forward, we watched hundreds of individual Army soldiers moving to the rear. Earlier, our section of the main line of resistance had become quiet; no enemy soldiers could be found forward of our position. Therefore, higher command had moved our battalion into another section of the line that was under attack by strong enemy forces.

During our initial movement forward by truck, I observed one soldier, then pairs of soldiers, and as we moved closer to the front, large groups of soldiers, all walking to the rear. These U.S. Army soldiers were all without weapons and all moving rearward with their heads down in spite of our barking and growling at them as we normally did when passing Army units. (Army soldiers were "doggies" to us Marines.)

This obviously unauthorized, disorganized movement to the rear did not lead me to be concerned about what we were moving into. In fact, I did not give it much thought at the time. My fellow 3rd Squad members did not have much respect for Army soldiers anyway, as too many times we had been tasked with taking hills that they could not gain or with holding positions that the higher commanders were concerned about losing. We were the Marines, the fire brigade. We were called upon to do what others could not. If I had feared what we were moving into, these hundreds of "bug outs" surely would have fed the flames of my fear. These were not only my thoughts; as other squad members openly expressed the same feelings regarding the situation.

I believe that a negative attitude was the major problem within the Army unit's ranks; one soldier goes, then another, and eventually they all move away from the threat. Idleness, no doubt, was a factor, but the big contributor to their fear must have been poor performance by others and faith or confidence in themselves or their unit. Other factors at play may have included: a lack of teamwork among the individuals, voiced negative opinions, and negative personal thoughts. These factors all feed fear.

Shortages of support, personnel, and equipment tend to feed fear, though shortages are seldom a problem for the Army. If we do not have what is needed to complete a job, we are naturally concerned. Exhaustion feeds fear in the same manner. Having done too much already does not leave any energy in reserve. When one is short in what is needed to accomplish the mission, fear is fed and reinforced.

Lack of faith or belief in the cause, unit, and/or leader feeds fear as well. The Army personnel walking to the rear probably lacked faith. They were all African-Americans except for their commander, who we met a little further down the road. He had eagles on his collar, indicating he was a full colonel, and he was white. Though he was the commanding officer, he clearly was not a part of the unit. He was not with his troops but sitting in his jeep alongside of the road as we moved forward. Where was he and what was his location the previous night in reference to his soldiers on the front line?

Having to work with and live with fear is bad enough.

We do not want to make it worse by feeding that fear. Being aware of what is contributing to any fearful situation gives one the chance to cut it off, to stop the feeding. Then, we hope, the fear can be handled.

Handling Fear

One might gather that fear is best handled with the use of courage. Again, I believe courage is the most beneficial personality trait one can have. One without courage tends to fall short in many other ways. An individual without, or short on, courage will quickly take the easiest way out and compromise his or her integrity rather than face the facts, the expense or the burden of truth. We see it among some of our politicians in positions of leadership. But then, I suppose it is all about and has to do with what the meaning of "is" is. Without courage, fear overcomes and causes the person to take the course of action that will not be as demanding of him or her.

The following list provides some of the ways I have found to handle fear:

1. Action is a great help: get moving. (In combat, offensive action provides less time for thoughts that bring on fear than manning defensive positions.)
2. Be qualified and prepared for the task.
3. Believe in the cause or action.
4. Know your people, both team members and leaders.
5. Have confidence in yourself and your team.
6. Have pride in yourself and your team.
7. Recognize that you will face your team members tomorrow.
8. Repeat the action as soon as possible. (This is especially true following a physical injury. As the old saying goes, "If you fall off the horse, get right back on.")

As expressed earlier, I believe that a person's character determines how well he or she will handle fear.

At this point, I must acknowledge one of the greatest examples of courage in our nation's history. Our countrymen and women exemplified with their actions the fullest meaning of the word in their handling of a direct attack on our freedom and way of life. I refer to the passengers of United Flight 93, which crashed on a farm in Pennsylvania on September 11, 2001.

We have all seen, heard, and read about the horrific events that took place that day. Our news media promptly and with great detail provided us with pictures and words to illustrate what was taking place. On that day, the terrorists were successful with their primary objective of instilling fear in Americans. But they, the terrorists, did not allow for the American fighter and today's means of personal communications, which allow us to fight back and against the fear.

For all we know, there were courageous responses in all four hijacked planes that morning. We will never know what took place on the first three planes, whose passengers and crew did not know they were part of a coordinated attack. From outside of the situation, we can only imagine what took place in the air on all four flights, but the last plane ended up differently from the other three.

Some passengers on United Flight 93 received advance warning that terrorist could have commandeered their flight by cell phone messages from family members and friends who had heard about the World Trade Center and Pentagon attacks earlier that morning. Thus some passengers on United Flight 93 may have suspected their plane could be attacked. There is not a doubt in my mind that one or more of our countrymen showed great leadership at this stage. I imagine they inspired their fellow passengers with words similar to, "Come on guys, they cannot cut all of us at once. All together now! Get them! Smother them on the deck with our bodies! Place your knee where it hurts him the most! Kill them before they kill us all!"

Although we will never know the details of the courageous acts that took place on United Flight 93, we know that the passengers managed to keep the terrorists from hitting their intended target. Fear had to be foremost in the minds of everyone aboard the plane, but they handled it through action. They took the fight to the enemy with the now-famous words, "Let's roll!"

Action has always been my method for handling fear, as it helps me in several ways. First, it keeps me busy reasoning, planning, and working out the solution rather than thinking about and fearing the consequences. The active brain considers how to respond to the situation, the steps to go through, and the major points to be on guard against. Action gets one moving and out of the mental-freeze zone. Action gets the blood flowing to and through the brain and with that can come more reaction plans.

Courageous responses handle our fears, and we pull these responses from within ourselves and from others around us. Gaining from and borrowing from others involved with us is what makes the team so important to us in fearful situations.

4

Boot Camp

PERHAPS THE WORD *FEAR* does not describe my reaction to my worst boot camp experience, but the words *anticipation* and *awareness of danger* to the achievement of my goals surely fit. Moreover, fear's synonym *dread* was very much a part of my final personnel and rifle inspection, which was conducted by an officer. I had never seen a Marine Corps officer at Parris Island, let alone been inspected by one. Corporal D. W. Reiser, my senior drill instructor, was right up there beside God in deciding whether I lived or died. If a corporal had that much authority, this officer could easily have wiped me off the face of the earth—no questions asked.

On this October morning in 1950, the sun was bright and hot; it was directly to the front of our platoon, which was standing in ranks for the inspection. While the brightness of the sun was uncomfortable for us, the Marine recruits, it was to the advantage of the inspecting officer. Positioned at his back, it aided in his scrutiny of the subjects before him.

As I was in the 3rd Squad, I had about an hour to harbor the discomfort of that hot sun plus dread and anticipation that the worst would happen when the inspector came to me. I tried to hear what he was asking the recruits in the 1st and 2nd squads in front of me, but he did not speak loudly enough for that, probably on purpose. He was physically sharp, and he performed with perfection as he smacked the M-1 rifle from each recruit's hand after positioning himself, with smart facing movements, militarily in front of them.

A recruit in the 1st Squad did not answer the captain's question correctly and received much physical and verbal abuse from both the officer and Corporal Reiser. The captain's second question went unanswered, as the recruit stood there in apparent shock. I heard the officer's third question, which was, "What is the name of your drill instructor?" The recruit did not answer; the captain threw the rifle at the recruit and moved away in obvious disgust. I began to think the worst: Would I know the answer to his questions? Would I do the rifle manual of arms correctly?

My body was getting stiff and pains were shooting through my limbs from standing at parade rest all of this time. I wondered if I could even move my rifle, let alone go through the manual for inspection arms, which ended with a hit of my left thumb against the operating rod handle to place the bolt in the open position.

There was not a doubt in my mind that I was afraid. Not only did I dread what was moving slowly and surely toward me, I was chocked-full of fear. I knew I would walk away with my life, but I wanted with all my heart to be a Marine. For all I knew, this inspection would decide that outcome. I wanted to do well, to convince this Marine officer that I was worthy of joining his ranks. I recognized my fear.

I feared the unknown in this final command personnel and rifle inspection. Drill instructor's inspections were bad and included physical and verbal abuse. I didn't know that an officer's inspection would not go to that depth. It seemed to me that because officers were higher in rank than our corporal, their inspections had to be worse. I expected verbal and physical abuse if I did not complete my inspection arms movements smartly and correctly, and I could see confirmation of my worst fears taking place with recruits going before me.

Negative personal thoughts fed my fear during that miserable hour of waiting for the slow-moving officer to reach me. My negative thoughts about what to expect from that officer, who would likely drag me through the coals, were reinforced by what I observed taking place within the two squads in front of me. I did not dare look at the inspector, but I did not miss much of what was going on before me.

One poor recruit in the 2nd Squad gave a sloppy inspection arms movement, and I thought the captain would kill him. While the captain did not strike the recruit, he may as well have, given all of the fuss he made. A barrage of questions, to which the recruit could not respond, followed, and he ended up crying as the inspector left him in vocal disgust with the words, "Shithead! You do not have and will never have what it takes to be a Marine! Get out of my sight!"

Standing there in ranks at parade rest (which is never a rest), becoming stiffer and stiffer, I felt that I could not move my arms, let alone do the movements of the rifle inspection. I did not know about everything in the world, and this inspector seemed to expect that of us. My dread reached its height as he finished with the 2nd Squad and moved on to my squad, where I was number three from the lead.

It was tough enough as the inspector worked over my squad leader, but when he positioned himself in front of the recruit on my right, my world was fast coming to an end. I could not see how I could continue with this madness. The negative thoughts feeding my fear were allowing it to take over.

But action helped me handle that fear. Though I was stiff with expectation and fear while the captain worked over the recruit to my right, the instant he moved in front of me, I was moving. The stiffness departed as I smacked my M-1 rifle as if I wished it were the captain's head. All my movements were precise and exact; I had instant relief from the fear that I might mess up.

The captain smacked the rifle away from me, and my hands dropped instantly to my side. He twirled my rifle, pausing while he searched it as if he were going over every inch with a magnifying glass. At this point, I was certain that he would not find a speck of dirt, dust, grease, or anything else. I knew my rifle was spotless; it was an extension, if not a part, of me. The physical action had calmed me down, and my brain was functioning and ready for his questions, which followed immediately.

"Recruit, what is the zero of your range rifle at five hundred yards?"

"Sir, the zero of this recruit's range rifle at five hundred yards is eighteen elevation and four left windage, Sir!"

That one was right down my alley; I knew my rifle and everything about it. Confidence took over. I was going to be a Marine!

"Who is the Commandant of the Marine Corps?"

"Sir, the Commandant of the Marine Corps is General Clifton B. Cates, Sir!"

The captain seemed pleased and returned my rifle. As he did his right face in his movement to my left, I closed the bolt, pulled the trigger, and snapped to order arms. Much personal practice with my rifle, going through the inspection arms movements, helped me handle my fear with the knowledge that I could succeed in that part of the inspection. But,

I have to admit that I lucked out on the questions asked. I was keenly aware that I did not know everything on the tactical and technical side that recruits were taught and expected to know.

5

The Korean War

IN JANUARY 1951, I JOINED 3rd Squad, 3rd Platoon, Item Company, 3rd Battalion, 5th Marine Regiment, 1st Marine Division in the Korean War. I was a gung-ho Marine (correction: I *am* a gung-ho Marine), but I was also a lucky Marine in my early days in that war. With no infantry training worthy of the word, this private first class found himself on the cutting edge in Korea as a member of a Marine rifle squad. Further, I asked for and received the Browning automatic rifle (BAR), a heavy responsibility for an individual. The BARman was next senior to the fire team leader, his weapon was the only automatic rifle in the fire team, and all action revolved around and in support of the BARman. The lifespan of a BARman in a firefight during World War-II was said to be less than a minute as the source of automatic weapon fire is a prime target for the enemy.

In our early assaults on those Korean ridgelines, I was usually the first Marine through the enemy defensive obstacles, if there were any, and the first Marine on top of the hill or ridgeline. Having little to no infantry training, I did what I had seen John Wayne do in the movies. I was lucky because the Chinese and North Korean soldiers had vacated the hilltops as we launched our assault. They usually left the objective during the air assault by our close air support Marines with F4U Corsair fighter/bombers. I liked this Marine rifleman business.

In April 1951, my squad leader, Cpl Myron Davis, moved me into one of his fire team leader positions. Reluctantly, I had to give up my BAR and carry an M-1 rifle, but it was not a bad position for a private first class five months out of boot camp. I had a lot to learn, and it would dump on me fast. Handling fear was part of my learning experience. Up to this point I had not been involved in any heavy firefights. The enemy was in full retreat. At this point, however, his retreat stopped, and the enemy force counterattacked all along the United Nations forces' main line of resistance.

Suspicious Sounds Forward

Being new at your job, having limited tools of trade, and having to react to the unknown can cause a high level of stress, if not fear. I experienced this one night on one of those Korean ridgelines in April 1951. The night was pitch-black with absolutely no visibility. The crickets and other night insects made their sounds, but one grows accustomed to that. My ears were listening for strange sounds, or maybe not strange, but sounds that were made by man.

Having recently assigned me the position of fire team leader, my squad leader gave me my team's area to cover and left it to me to assign my men their fighting positions. As it turned out, the frontline area assigned to my fire team was so wide that our fighting positions were seventy-five yards apart in some places, as were the rest of the squad's individual positions. Once again we were faced with the old problem of how two to four Marines could stop and hold an enemy assault of several hundred soldiers. And, the problem was compounded because we had no advance warning; we knew they were there only when they hit us, face to face. There could be no reduction of the enemy force with long-range fire and supporting weapons.

I wanted my Browning automatic rifleman and his assistant together, so they were assigned to one hole. Because of the terrain features, if my rifleman and I shared the second position, we would not have daytime visual contact with one of our flank positions. Of course, darkness compounded this problem and was my primary concern. I decided that the better plan was for the two of us to have separate fighting positions. This, during daylight at least, gave us visual contact in both directions along the line. It was not ideal, but then, neither was the width of our squad and platoon frontage. Of course, the entire rifle company line was likewise strung out and in no better defensive posture.

My rifleman and I would have to share our watch with one of us awake at all times between the two holes. We normally stood watch for one hour and then slept for one hour when together in one position. Now, the watch stander had to move about thirty yards in the dark on that rough hillside to pass the watch duty. I decided that we would handle it by taking two-hour watches, which worked well as the enemy was not lying in wait for us as we moved between our positions.

Sometime during my second watch, fear paid me a visit. In the total darkness with the insect sounds around me, I heard a strange noise in front of me and down the hill. We had just occupied and set in on this position late the evening before, and we did not have wire or any other barriers or signaling devices in front of us. (We didn't have the material even if we had had the time to install it. In addition, we were to maintain this position only one night, as we were in the attack.) Straining to identify the sound and location and to see through the total darkness, I determined that the sounds were coming from something or someone walking in the leaves. Was this an enemy patrol? Or, worse yet, was it the advance of an enemy assault?

There were several causes of the concern and apprehension building up in me: Our one-man position was part of it as was the fact that this was one of those very dark nights with no visibility. I could not see a thing except the blackness of the night. My rifleman in the next hole did not hear the movement or noise; he was asleep. If it were enemy movement, I needed to awaken him. Did my Browning automatic rifleman or his assistant, whoever was on watch, hear the noise? Were they ready to fight?

The noise was clear to me and appeared to be getting closer. Was an animal making it or was it a man or men? We had noticed wild hogs and deer feeding near our positions at other times. However, the more I listened, the more I was convinced that these were man-made sounds. One or more men of the enemy force was stumbling in the total darkness while walking through the leaves on the steep hillside in front of my position.

Several sources fed this fear within me: the realizations that I was alone, that I had no manner of quietly communicating with anyone (calling by radio for artillery or mortar illuminations rounds to be fired forward of my position for visibility), and that there was no ready source of assistance near my position.

I pulled the pin on a grenade and tossed it lightly so that it would roll down the hill toward the noise. The grenade exploded and the noise of feet became much louder and obvious. I heard multiple noises seemingly from many feet. I became more concerned and, yes, afraid. I knew the enemy was forward of me, and I needed light in order to target them with my rifle. My fire team and squad members had to know that we were under attack. Where in our squad frontage was the enemy's main thrust headed? My fear was being fed big time!

The only communication method available to alert my squad and platoon leaders was word of mouth. My platoon leader had to call by radio for mortar or artillery illumination to be fired over us so that we could see well enough to eliminate the threat. I reasoned that my squad needed the light and had to be alerted to the enemy's presence, even if it drew the danger to me. Though it would give away my position to the enemy, I decided to yell for illumination and hope that the lieutenant or someone on watch in the command post on the ridgeline above heard me. I yelled, "Give me lum forward!" I yelled several times before the light was fired over me.

The noise went away shortly after the flares went up. It could have been several wild hogs, or maybe my yelling scared off the enemy. But, I doubt that my voice sounded like that of a Marine warrior.

If the noise was enemy footsteps, I had little to loose by yelling: I was in their path with or without the flares. I really had no choice but to yell. Marines go down fighting, and I would take some enemy with me. I wanted to see my targets. Also, my rifleman was my responsibility; he was sleeping in my trust.

Following the Chinese Night Attack

The Chinese night attack against my squad on the night of May 19, 1951, provided me with a new and different perspective on combat and fear. Rain showers had fallen throughout the day and continued through the night. Heavy clouds prevented any celestial lighting, and I could not see my hand if I held it in front of my face. The Chinese had managed to move behind me without my knowing for certain that they were on our ridgeline. With no light to assist in observation, such maneuvers could happen. Because of the close combat action that followed for the remainder of the night, I was not much aware of fear at the time. I was too busy taking care of the Chinese and staying alive.

Though many high-stress situations cropped up that night, the fear that I describe here came later the next evening and the following night. Most of fear's synonyms—dread, fright, alarm, trepidation, anxiety, irresolution, and nervousness—fit my situation, and the bottom line was I was afraid for my life. I have never been more fearful of an expected event than I was on the evening of May 20, 1951. Though I am not a pessimist, it was clear to me that if the Chinese hit us here, I didn't have a chance.

On the morning of the twentieth, my squad was pulled out of the line for rest and reorganization as a result of the casualties we had suffered in our fight the night before. I really needed that time, especially the chance for sleep—a long, uninterrupted sleep with no watches. We sat around the platoon command post for what seemed like forever while someone decided what to do with us, and then we were moved back on the line. This time, though, instead of being on the line, we extended our position forward down a feeder ridge or finger into no-man's-land.

As if the extension forward was not bad enough, I was assigned to the last fighting position down the ridge, the forward-most position of the squad. All other squad members were lined up in holes thirty to forty yards apart and extending behind me to the top of the ridge and the main line of resistance. Of course we were in two-man positions, but having one Marine beside me was not much help against hundreds of Chinese soldiers. My squad members could not fire forward without hitting us in the back, so there could be no unity of effort, no maximum squad defensive fire forward.

The Chinese assault the previous night had come up a draw to our right; on this night, they could come right up this ridge finger. Of course we were placed there to stop just such an action. This was probably a good tactic considering the overall picture—a good defense of the main line of resistance—but it meant certain death for the two most forward individuals, of which I was one.

I could not believe my lousy luck—no sleep last night and little promise of sleep this night. I felt that I did not have a chance if the enemy attacked, and I knew an attack was going to happen. I have never been more consumed by fear and all that goes with it. I was on a heavy down swing, but I would learn shortly after dark that my fear had not yet bottomed out. Again, I recognized a fear.

My fear sprang from several causes, not the least of which was exhaustion. I had been out on a listening post for the first half of that rainy night prior, with no sleep, obviously. We then fought for the rest of the night. Dread and anxiety describe what I experienced that evening of the twentieth. My squad's positions extended from the main defensive line forward with absolutely no flank security for any of our squad fighting holes. We did not have a chance of surviving another enemy assault; the lives of everyone in the squad were in great danger.

The Chinese and North Korean soldiers could and would take us on one by one, with me being first. The only time squad members behind me could fire on enemy soldiers to my front would be when I was below ground in my hole, and how would they know I had taken cover in the dark? And, how could I cover and defend my position forward while down in my hole? My buddies could not help me.

I thought that my spirit and morale could not get any lower, but I had much yet to learn. As I mentioned earlier, our squad had been reorganized that morning because of casualties taken. Third Platoon had lost three Browning automatic riflemen during the night fight, and those key positions were filled by other riflemen within the platoon. My fire team rifleman was moved to another fire team, where he took over the Browning automatic rifleman position. His replacement in my team had been with us for my entire time in Korea. He had served in rifleman positions with other squads and more recently had been one of the platoon runners. I thought I knew him and had no problem with his assignment to my team from the platoon command post.

Because this story portrays this individual in a negative light, I will call him Private First Class Vinyard, not his actual name. He left me for a trip to the command post while we were preparing our fighting position; he had to see a corpsman. His departure was not a problem as our hole was dug, and I was finishing up clearing our field of fire. He returned just before darkness fell.

I set up our watch schedule and talked about the way I expected us to handle the night, including any probe by or approach of the enemy. The person on watch had to be alert to any unusual sounds and activity. Vinyard had been in the command post the night before and not involved in our firefight, so I told him that I was exhausted and needed sleep. He should make sure that I was awake each time he turned the one-hour watch shift over to me. "Don't just nudge me and then go to sleep," I said.

Vinyard responded, "Not a problem. I don't need sleep."

"What do you mean you 'don't need sleep'?"

He said, as he extended his hand, "Here, take one of these, and you won't need sleep, either. You just don't worry about things."

I did not want to believe what I heard or saw: this dope-head was on morphine. That explained Vinyard's close relationship with a certain corpsman (who carried morphine in those days for the wounded when needed) and displays of strength and endurance. He was a small man in both weight and height, and I had earlier marveled that he was always messing about when the rest of us were exhausted on the side of the road or trail during a hard movement.

One example of Vinyard's energy came during one of our movement breaks, when we sat or lay exhausted along the roadside. Vinyard moved among us extending his carbine with bayonet attached around and into the face of individual Marines. With the hand of a cadaver stuck on his bayonet, he would come up from behind a Marine. His sick purpose was to get a rise from his buddies; most of us did not think the act was funny. Yet, he walked around at sling arms for days with that hand still on his bayonet.

I refused the drug offer and realized that I was in that fighting hole alone. This guy was absolutely of no help to me, the squad, or the platoon. I could not depend on his senses, his thought process, or any other part of him. I was on watch for the entire night. I woke him for his one-hour watches, and I crawled into my sleeping bag, but I did not sleep. I dozed some, but I always knew that he was awake. In addition, my ears were attuned to any activity outside of our hole. This character helped feed my fear in a major way.

I got through the night of May 20 in no-man's-land with the dopehead. While I didn't sleep that night, for the second night running, recovering my rest thereafter wasn't a problem. My squad received no patrol activity; during daylight we sat around, ate c-rations, talked to each other, prepared our defensive positions, and slept. Rest was a great help but what really assisted me in handling my fear in this situation is spelled out below: being prepared.

I prepared my position forward so that even a squirrel could not have approached me without my knowledge. I took a dozen hand grenades, tied them to trees near areas that were open enough to be a route for someone moving by foot up the hill, straightened the pin in the fuse, tied communication wire to the ring, ran the wire across the open space, and tied the other end to a bush or tree. Anyone or anything hitting the wire would pull the pin from the fuse, and in four seconds the grenade would explode. An alert individual had four seconds to hit the deck or move away, but I would be alerted to his presence nevertheless by the grenade explosions.

Work that really made me feel good, that downgraded my fear to a manageable level, was rigging an old fighting hole about thirty yards down the hill from my position and in the center of the ridge. Enemy personnel would most likely walk right up the ridge, hitting this hole first. I rigged up a dummy sitting in the hole, put a helmet on its head, and placed a stick to appear as a rifle sloping across its front in the port arms or ready position. I was convinced that during darkness this would look enough like a Marine in his fighting hole to get the enemy's attention. When they assaulted this dummy hole, I would open up with rifle fire while also showering the area with hand grenades.

Action handled my fear in several ways. It gave me something to do, occupied my mind in a worthwhile way, and reduced the time available to worry. Belief in my defensive measures helped greatly. The booby-trapped hand grenades and the dummy in the hole were instrumental in my peace of mind; I had confidence in what they would do for me. Staying awake all night with one eye on my foxhole "buddy" ceased to be a major problem; my fear was handled and reduced.

Assault on an Enemy Machine Gun

My squad's assault on a North Korean machine-gun position on June 8, 1951, gave me an eyeball-to-eyeball confrontation with fear, and I quickly recognized it as such. The action was during Item Company's third assault on the main ridgeline that day and our 3rd Platoon's second assault on this particular ridge, which had resulted in our taking two intermediate objectives on the way up. A heavy machine gun had stopped our assault, and we had to deal with that problem.

The sky was clear enough to allow Marine close air support, and we had our fighter/bombers working over the enemy position prior to our assault. My squad was to launch our assault on the enemy position under cover of the last two planes' dive on the position. These were dummy runs designed to give us an advantage by keeping the enemy soldiers pinned down as we moved forward.

We had been in the attack for weeks with little sleep at night and limited rations. Squad members were exhausted and the casualties taken earlier that morning were a major role in weakening our Marine warrior mentality. Most Marines probably felt as I did, that we weren't ready to do what had to be done. Reorganization within our platoon immediately prior to this assault necessitated some major mental adjustments, at least with me. We had seven Marines in the squad at this point (down from the thirteen of a full squad). Four of the seven were corporals, the squad leader was Cpl. Orville L. Miller (Davis had completed his tour of duty and returned home) and the fire team leader was Cpl. James B. Roop. Cpl. Bob Levangie and I (being the junior corporals) ended up with no team members as there were none left. Our platoon leader, Lt. Donald R. Brimmer, during his assault briefing to the squad, designated Levangie and I as the point in our assault on the gun. (Normally, the squad leader assigns his squad member's roles in the assault.)

Third Squad's assault formation on the gun was a single file that amounted to a one-man front, as we were lined up one behind the other, ten to fifteen yards apart staggered up the ridgeline. I was first and Bob was close behind me. Initially, my 3rd Squad's assault worked as planned, in spite of a late and half-hearted movement when the time came for our part of the action. The last plane was in its dive before we even started our move forward.

Personally, my movement up that hill in the assault was anything but aggressive. The Marine instinct and drive in me was not working well that day; there were just too many unknowns in this situation. The effects of the unknowns were compounded by the fact that our squad had reorganized because of casualties taken earlier that morning, which included the loss of friends, Marine buddies.

I was almost on the ridge when the enemy machine gun opened fire on the squad members strung out behind me down the finger. The North Korean soldiers had left the ridge during the air strike by Marine F4U Corsairs. They returned to their guns a minute or two before me, and they opened fire. I ran through napalm fire and smoke to get out of their kill zone and, in effect, skirted their forward defensive fire and observation. Pausing behind an eight-inch or so diameter pine tree to assess my situation, I realized that I was alone on the ridge with the enemy.

Taking on the entire North Korean Army, alone, was a monumental enterprise for this teenager. But I had to do it because that machine gun was killing my squad buddies down the hill from me. I experienced fear, great fear. I knew that I was afraid of facing what was ahead of me, but there was not a question in my mind about doing it. The major cause of my fear was that, again, I was placed in a difficult situation for which I was unprepared and unqualified. I was about to do what my buddies and I had done as kids while playing soldier—assault the enemy. But it would not be "bang, bang, you're dead" and get up to play some more. This action was real.

I was keenly aware that I had no team or buddy support for the task facing me. The enemy machine gun had separated me from my squad members, and, for all I knew, they were all dead or dying. My platoon leader and the rest of my platoon were on the ridge behind me, where my squad had left them when we moved forward for our assault. That heavy machine-gun fire had my full attention.

There was no time for anything to feed my fear. Now was the time for action. I moved from the tree. One second I was moving against the gun, and the next thing I knew, I regained consciousness far down the ridge.

The grenade that took me out relieved me of the task of handling my recognized fear. I have to admit that I felt a major load lifted off of me when I regained consciousness down that hill from the enemy gun. I was no longer in a position to take it on, to knock it out. Also, I was unarmed. I no longer had my rifle, and I felt naked without it. Somehow my pack had come off my back during my unconscious roll down that steep hill and was missing. I moved up the hill to where I expected to find the rear of my squad. During my attempt to acquire another rifle, I was directed by my platoon leader to see a corpsman. Shortly thereafter I was medevaced off the ridgeline by helicopter because I had several shrapnel wounds. (I never learned what happened to Bob; however, he is not listed in the unit's after action reports as a casualty along with me and others for that day.)

In hindsight and with my ideas on action helping to handle fear, I should not have paused behind that pine tree. That gave me time to think about the dangers before me while I considered how I was going to knock out that gun. At that point, the enemy gun had been over the crest of the ridge, on the side of the hill, and on my left flank; I couldn't see it. If I had continued moving toward the gun rather than pausing to think and get my bearings, maybe I could have knocked it out. At least I would have had a better chance.

Late June 1951 Ridgeline Defense

The United Nations' assault north ceased with our capture of good defensive ground inside the North Korean boundary just north of the 38th Parallel in late June 1951. Peace talks continued between the major countries involved in the war. At this time, my rest, a full night's sleep every night, and good food at the medical battalion ended when my wounds healed well enough for me to return to my squad. I rejoined them, and Item Company dug in on defensive positions along the southern ridges of what was known as the Punch Bowl.

As we were in a defensive posture, we did not do much once we had prepared our positions. There were patrol actions, but we had a lot of time to do nothing. Our company had been in the assault mode since May 23 and though we Marines were physically well-worn if not always exhausted, movement and action had occupied our minds. Now, it was a different story, a different situation. Our mission changed from offense to defense—and defense is never a desirable role for Marines. Instead of being in the assault and taking the ridge-lines, we were now committed to holding a ridgeline against a probable enemy attack. I realize as I write this that the cause of the fear I experienced with the coming of night was my lack of infantry training. This stuff was all new to me, and lately, I had come to realize just how little I knew about taking the fight to the enemy. Basically, I was unprepared and unqualified to do what I was there to do.

Because I lacked effective infantry training and tactical knowledge, I found myself placed in a difficult situation. I felt that expectations of me and the members of my squad were higher than normal and unreasonable. My confidence in the little training I did get was shaken by the Chinese assault on May 20, during which not only had the enemy reached my squad's ridge but the force was also behind me before I even knew for sure that we were under attack. It does not get any worse. And if they did it once, they could do it again. How could we defend our positions when we could not see the enemy to target him during his approach to our positions?

Each afternoon around 1500, when the sun would start sinking in the west, if I were not on patrol, I would begin worrying about the coming night and whether I would be able to see in the dark. Would it be another completely black night with absolutely no visibility? It was during the rainy season, and if there were clouds, there would be no moon or stars, no luminosity, no light at all. If I allowed the thoughts to build, I would become close to sick with dread. Was my problem dread or fear? Is there a difference when your life is at stake? This feeling of concern, dread, anxiety, danger, distress, worry, trepidation, and whatever else one would call it, amounted to fear. All of these words fit my feelings, and I was very much bothered from the effect.

Several factors fed my fear. Probably the main contributor was the idleness that gave me too much time to think. This free time allowed my mind to wonder, to dream up situations, to imagine the worst, and to build up my anxiety level.

Other than patrol actions, we did next to nothing. We built small fires on the reverse side of the hill to warm c-rations and make coffee. We had plenty of bull sessions around our little fires and we came to know each other better, but talking with fellow Marines did not take my mind off my worries as the day came to an end. The awareness of another night coming upon me within a few hours would renew my fear of having no visibility. Total darkness allowed the enemy to be on me before I could react in defense.

Another factor feeding this fear was the shortage of Marines for the area we were defending. The distances between our two-man fighting positions were so large that on a dark night, the enemy could easily move through our defense by centering a small force between our fighting positions. In a few places we had 80 to 100 yards between our fighting holes, and in some of these areas, terrain features, such as huge rocks, gullies, and vegetation, ensured that the enemy could move unobserved.

How could two, maybe six of us at the most, hold off and stop a force numbering in the hundreds that spearheaded at a single spot in our line of defense, especially if the night was so dark that you could not see your own nose? We could not take the enemy under fire and deplete his force before he reached our positions. And having time to think about these problems did not help my mental situation.

I learned to handle my fear with my recent experience, faith, and combat support from other units. Clear nights were not a concern; if the moon and stars were out, all was well. Heavily clouded nights and nights with rain were the problem. But we had no weather forecaster in our squad, no newspaper with weather information, and, of course, no radio. We knew it was going to rain when the rain fell, which was quite often.

*The author as a squad leader on a Korean
ridgeline during the war in 1951*

*The author's buddy Shelton Lee Eakin in cold
weather clothing in Korea in 1954.*

The author's wife, Dotti Lu, the lady with the eagle, globe, and anchor heart.

The author in the field at Khe Sanh, Vietnam with his rifle company.

The author at his command post in the Vietnam jungle, controlling his rifle company's actions.

Right to left: the author, 1st Lieutenant Albert Sheppard, 2nd Lieutenant William Christman, and 2nd Lieutenant James Davis with Company A, 1st Battalion, 9th Marines. The Marines are in taking a break while deployed in the field, Vietnam.

An example of what can go wrong during a parachute operation. Here Lt. Cpl. Dennis Boyle, 1st Force Reconnaissance Company, is hung up outside of his jump plane, a C-1A, in the Philippines in 1962. He survived and landed well.

Two surplus-modified parachute canopies with a "TU" cut out of the gores.

*The Cessna jump plane, which requires
a crawl out and hang on the strut to jump.*

The author in the jump door of a C-1A.

The author just outside of the aircraft door.

The author in free fall, flat and stable.

The author gives jump master safety checks
to his jumpers prior to jumping.

The author under a square parachute. He has just released his
equipment bag for his landing. This was one of the testing and
evaluation jumps he made while performing the duties of the
reconnaissance officer, Development Center, Quantico, Virginia.

The author in an easy exit, just off the ramp of a CH-46.

The unknown fed my fear because I never knew what we were getting until darkness fell. But this problem went away.

For whatever reason—because we were holding key terrain the higher commanders did not want to lose, or because it was our turn to get support, or because the Army did not need it anywhere else—we got light. After a few days of worrying about the coming darkness, the Army placed huge searchlights in the valleys behind us, and on those dark nights, aimed them upward and forward to bounce off the clouds. The heavier the cloud cover, the better our artificial light. On rainy nights, like the one on May 20 when there was absolutely no visibility, those searchlights gave us light equal to that of a full moon. I could see well ahead of and down the hill from my position. We could and would cut down any assault force in front of us with little possibility of any enemy troops gaining our positions. My dread of the coming darkness went away; we were prepared for the task.

We used our own work, efforts, and ingenuity to ease our concern about a sneak attack by placing many early warning devices in front of our position. Our supply of barbed wire was limited, but we made good use of what came our way. We used empty c-ration cans (of which there was no shortage) with small pebbles placed in them and tied them to wire and bushes so that they would make noise when someone hit or touched the wire or bush. Our other early warning devices included trip flares and booby-trapped grenades forward and down the hill from our position. Even with no searchlights, the enemy would have had a difficult time getting to us without our knowing it.

Having so much time in position, we were able to prepare for the enemy's attack. Keeping busy in this way helped us fend off fear by the use of action and preparedness. And, always we had the support and faith of our leaders, which helped greatly in handling fears of the type we experienced in Korea.

6

The Vietnam War

FEAR PAID A MAJOR VISIT to me during my rifle company's action against a North Vietnamese bunker defense on February 22, 1969. My company was Alpha of the 1st Battalion, 9th Marine Regiment, 3rd Marine Division. Our regiment was in the middle of Operation Dewey Canyon, which took place in the A Shau Valley, Quang Tri Province, Vietnam. The A Shau Valley runs along the Laotian border and had been, up to this time, a safe haven for the enemy. My regimental commander, Col. Robert H. Barrow, and my battalion commander, Lt. Col. George W. Smith, interfered with the North Vietnamese Army's safe use of that area with this operation. Our regiment jumped off in the attack, and we stayed on the operation in excess of two months.

February 22 was a heavily overcast day with rain clouds right down in the trees providing intermittent showers; it was not a good day to be looking for the enemy if you expected you might need help from Marine air. My company combat patrol located the enemy force for which we had been searching and Alpha assaulted their position. The enemy force turned out to be in a bunker defense and provided automatic weapon fire so heavy that my two-platoon assault stalled. This was a larger and stronger force than my commander and I expected.

My company was very much under strength at the start of this assault because we had taken casualties in the prior four weeks of the operation and had received few replacements. We were further low in number because I had assigned one rifle squad to another mission about an hour before I found the enemy force. I had fewer than ninety Marines with me at this time. I had left my mortar section on the ridge with the battalion because I was moving, and I could not use them short of clearing areas of the jungle to do so. I was confident, however, that we could overcome the enemy resistance. I would commit my reserve platoon to the assault. At this stage I was too involved with my thoughts and action to be aware of fear, even though earlier a rocket-propelled grenade had exploded against a bush beside me, hitting me with shrapnel and giving me a slight concussion.

An enemy mortar round hit and exploded among us as I directed Lt. James Davis to take his rifle platoon into the attack, my platoon held in reserve. Lieutenant Davis had been badly wounded by shrapnel from the mortar round causing me to direct 1st Lt. Lee Roy Herron, my company executive officer, to take command of the 2nd Platoon. He had heard my assault order to Lieutenant Davis and was ready to go. Lee led the 2nd Platoon forward, and my Marines along the line were able to advance.

The incoming mortar round seriously wounded all three of my radio operators. Though hit with shrapnel for the second time that day myself, I now had three radios to handle—battalion command, my company command, and the artillery net. Seeing me overloaded with radios, one of my snipers, LCpl. Mike Winter, crawled over to me and took over one of the radios.

Within minutes of Winter's arrival at my forward position, machine-gun fire raked through us, nearly cutting down a tree only inches in front of us. Winter took a round through his right leg while the remaining rounds missed me. How did all those rounds miss me? We were pinned down in a small depression of the ground with a good-sized tree on the enemy side of our low spot and the source of machine-gun fire. Winter needed immediate medical help; I directed him to crawl over to Hospital Man Second Class (Doc) Charles Hudson, my company senior corpsman, who was busy tending to those wounded by the mortar round.

At this time, I received a radio call from each of my three platoon sergeants, one immediately following the other. Their platoon leaders were casualties. Sergeant Beyerlein of my 2nd Platoon was first with the word that Lieutenant Herron had been killed by machine-gun fire during their assault forward. First Platoon's SSgt. Robert Jenson and 3rd Platoon's Sgt. Michael Lane followed with the facts that their platoon leaders—Lt. George Malone and Lt. William Christman, respectively—were severely wounded and out of the fight. (Christman died before our fight was over.)

The enemy machine gun located me again and continued shooting at a heavy rate of fire that cut up the foliage and ground around me. I knew fear at that moment; I had all I could handle. All of my platoon leaders were out of the fight. Even though my platoon sergeants were competent gunfighters, and I had full confidence in their abilities to fight their platoons, I was fast becoming short of Marines.

The enemy machine gun had to be taken out, but how? I could not get my head up to assess the situation because bullets cut through the jungle growth and ground around me. A deep hole that I could have crawled into and closed behind me would have suited my mental state at that moment. I recognized fear in a big way. The loss of my platoon leaders, the feeling of hopelessness caused by the lack of forward action, and the ugliness of the weather were all contributing factors. Nothing was going right.

If that machine gun could have placed its rounds one inch lower, it would have had me. I knew that my life was hanging on the edge. Yes, I felt fear. I felt fear because I was unable to react, to do anything about that machine gun. My mind and brain were functioning, and I considered several possibilities for action. But they all began with knocking out that machine gun. How? I hoped, some of my Marines were not under direct fire and were moving on it.

Each Marine was involved with his individual firefight against the enemy soldiers to his direct front, all separate actions in that dense jungle. I needed to be actively involved, to assess the situation and control our collective efforts. We needed a forward focus, a concerted three-platoon effort to knock out the enemy force command center. There was no way I could do anything in this position with that machine gun's fire over me. How was this situation going to end?

The helplessness of being pinned down in that depression by that machine gun fed my fear and was more than I wanted to handle. Feeding my fear also was the realization that I had to get moving, that my Marines needed direction, and that I could not influence the situation in our favor.

The enemy machine guns were across a somewhat open area with less underbrush, that provided good fields of fire. Further, the guns were quickly reducing the existing underbrush. Regardless of how I decided to take on the mission, it was going to cost me Marines. The fields of fire were just too good; the guns had my entire company pinned down. Maybe a flanking action would work, but I had to be able to move in order to get that or any action started. Did I have any

Marines close to it? The more I thought about the task facing me while I was unable to do anything about it, the more my fear was fed.

The North Vietnamese Army owned the day as long as their machine guns were rattling, placing rounds directly over me and my company. There may well have been more than one gun in that last position in front of me because we were under constant fire from several guns from the start of our assault. However, luck came to us and against our enemy. As mentioned, the day's weather had been a misty rain with low clouds; we had no close air support. But as I lay there in that depression, the clouds opened up with a big hole right above us—sunshine!

Fortunately, I had all radios with me in the depression, and I immediately called the battalion tactical radio net. My battalion commander, Lt. Col. George Smith, told me he had two OV-10 Bronco aircraft on station, just in case I could use them. Great! My commander was always thinking ahead and looking after his Marines. Getting the air radio frequency and call sign, I rolled my radio dials and shortly was talking with the flight leader. I was feeling better already, knowing my ground Marines might not have to take out that gun.

I gave the flight leader my grid coordinates, and he was overhead shortly. I directed my platoon sergeants to mark their forward position with smoke grenades, and I identified the enemy machine-gun positions to the flight leader with a magnetic azimuth and distance from the center of our smoke. The pilots were sharp and on the ball: their first rocket and machine-gun runs were directly on the enemy guns. The Bronco pilots continued their strafing runs for good measure and our firefight ended—no more machine guns, no more enemy. The courage of my ground Marines and those in the air handled my fear by eliminating its source.

7

Instructor Assignment

WHILE THERE IS A MAJOR DIFFERENCE between combat-induced fear and fear of something that is not life threatening, fear grips us even in peacetime situations. Experiencing fear's synonyms of *apprehension* and *dread* can cause more stress than is good for us. Being tasked to teach a class to Marines when I was a young sergeant in 1955 caused me such stress and concern. I had not received any training in how to teach, how to write a lesson outline, or how to put together a presentation. I did not want to waste my Marines' time—they should learn something from the class—and I surely did not want to be made fun of by salty Marines.

Noncommissioned officers learn to teach young Marines at the Noncommissioned Officers School, but I never had a chance to attend that school. Trying to prepare for a class was difficult for me, and I worried about my lesson plan for the several days before my presentation. Again, I recognized a fear.

Being untrained and technically unqualified to teach Marine Corps course material caused my apprehension and fear. Fear of public speaking was also part of it; I had no experience in giving a formal presentation to groups of people. Worse, I had to gain my Marines' attention, retain it, and teach the learning points of the particular subject correctly. The subjects did not cause me concern, as they were all Marine subjects, and I already had a comfortable knowledge of them. The mechanics of the presentation, how to write a lesson outline, and how to go about presenting it led to my anxiety about being an instructor.

When it comes to feeding this particular fear, I suppose the culprit was time. The more I thought about conducting the class and not knowing who to turn to for help with this assignment, my concern and apprehension grew.

Recognition of my duties and responsibilities as a non-commissioned officer, as a sergeant of Marines, helped me handle this stress, anxiety, and fear. I realized that instructor duty was an obligation of sergeants; we had to teach as well as train and guide our Marines. I sought help from my buddy, Sgt. Shelton Lee Eakin, who had recently graduated from the Noncommissioned Officers School. He had the know-how and the manuals, and he was already creating lesson plans of the highest quality.

I borrowed Eakin's manuals, took his advice, and sat in on his classes to better understand the details involved, including how to motivate and create a desire within your Marines to learn what you are tasked with teaching. Shortly, I was making up decent lesson outlines that allowed me to give my Marines high-quality instruction.

Being qualified and prepared for the task helps greatly to overcome fear, as it promotes belief and confidence in oneself. In time, my instructor assignment, once a cause of fear, became a pleasure.

Fort Benning

THE PEACETIME FEAR THAT CAME closest to comparing with my combat fears came during parachute jump training. Since I was a boy, I had wanted to be a paratrooper, as I had been impressed by an older cousin's involvement with the Special Service Force in World War II. At the Marine Recruiting Station, I was delighted to learn that the Marine Corps had the Paramarines. (This turned out to be incorrect information; the Paramarine unit was disbanded in 1944.) I really wanted to jump, to parachute from an aircraft in flight, but it would be ten years, 1960, before I could get into a Marine jump billet, in the recently established and organized 1st Force Reconnaissance Company, Fleet Marine Force, Pacific, located at Camp Pendleton, California.

All went well at Camp Pendleton during my 1st Force Reconnaissance Company acceptance and indoctrination training as well as during the initial parachute training on the ground at Fort Benning, Georgia, in April 1961. (The U.S. Army was tasked by the Defense Department to provided parachute training for all services at that time.) However, soon came the second week of training, tower week, during which we performed exercises on a thirty-four-foot jump tower.

Students wore a harness with risers attached for the jump out of the door at the top of the tower. The risers extended out to a dolly on a downward-sloped cable, which carried the student safely and easily down to the ground fifty yards away. One of the hardest things I have done in my life was to move to and leap out that door thirty-four feet above ground.

It was a beautifully warm spring day; everything had been moving in my favor. Up to this point in training, nothing had been difficult or had come even close to challenging my abilities. As a matter of fact, we four Marines in the class were constantly challenging the Army with their easy daily routine, especially in physical fitness. Airborne students were awarded ten push-ups for all minor infractions of the training routine. In paying off the award, students were required to yell "Airborne" as they dove to the deck for the push-ups. But we Marines sounded off with "Recon" on our way to the deck. For this infraction, we were awarded another set of ten push-ups for which we again yelled "Recon." The Army sergeants gave us a break after about ten sets of ten push-ups. The Army had a similarly easy running regimen: in jump school we ran only four minutes at a time with a two-minute walk in between two more four-minute runs. In Force Recon at Camp Pendleton, we ran forever!

My fear of the jump from the thirty-four-foot tower had a unique cause. Yes, I suppose I was afraid for my safety. One may assume that I did not trust the equipment or the Army sergeants, but that was not the case. The cause of my fear was probably all the time I had to think about what was ahead. The fact that the hard ground was thirty-four feet below, and for some reason, I thought I was going to hit it. My negative feelings started while I slowly climbed the stairs, one step at a time, as the jump students ahead of me leaped out the door, one and then another. With great difficulty, I moved slowly on the jump deck toward that door. Each student ahead of me had to be hooked up by one of the instructors for his jump, leaving me even more time to think about my fate.

Finally, after arriving at the door and having the instructor hook me to the cable, I jumped out on his command. But I did not present the desired body position as it was taught. In fact, the sergeant first class grading our body positions from the ground below was in stitches with laughter as I reported to him for his critique. I had messed it up so badly that all he could say, between peals of laughter, was, "Give me ten, Marine, and get back in line and do it again."

Not only did I not do anything correctly, but my fear must have been plastered all over my face. We had to have two good exits out of that tower before we went on to jump from a 250-foot tower and then an actual aircraft. After my first jump, I wondered if I could get it right, do it correctly. I finally mastered the thirty-four-foot jump tower, but it took many more than two jumps.

I found the 250-foot jump tower that was next in our training enjoyable as a result of the easy, relaxed manner in which that particular training was conducted. I only had one chance, one jump, at this tower. I was so comfortable with this jump that I wanted to do it again.

My first jump from an aircraft gave me another run-in with fear. Even though I was full of apprehension, dread, anxiety, and nervousness, I managed my feelings well enough while seated in the aircraft along with the other student jumpers. The jump could be called off because of wind or other safety reasons. I took comfort in the possibility that we might not jump; at the same time, however, I recognized my fear. The cause of this fear was facing the prospect of doing something that I had never done before, something that had cost others their lives.

The sticks (a group of parachutists exiting the aircraft together, one behind the other) were stood up, put through their equipment checks, lined up extending back from the open door, and, one by one, disappeared out that door. Damn, I thought, this jump is going to go! Still, I was not overly concerned. The jump could be cancelled even at this point; I understood it happened all the time. Nevertheless, time to think was feeding my fear; there was too much time to think of all the things that could go wrong. The emergency procedures we had practiced reinforced my thinking about all the problems one could experience while parachuting. Would my chute be the one that did not open? Would I be the one hung up outside of the aircraft? Would I respond properly to whatever happened?

Then, my stick received the signal to stand up. As we went through the equipment check, I began to feel less and less positive on what I was about to do. We sounded off with our number and "OK!" when directed, and number one moved to the door. Jumpers ahead of me started disappearing out of the door, and the remainder of our stick continued with forward movement. I had one huge, overriding thought: Why was I up here trying to kill myself? My life had been so good, so perfect up to this point. I had everything I wanted, or at least everything I needed. Why was I up here trying to throw it all away?

I was almost sick with fright as the jumper in front of me disappeared out of that door. I could see the big wide world outside sliding by below me. My hands went to the sides of the door, and I sprang out, feet together, hands covering the ends of my reserve parachute as I had been taught. Action caused my fear to stay in that C-123 aircraft.

A new experience that involved several unknowns was the main cause of those fears I experienced in jump school.

While I hesitate to use the word *major* to describe the fear I had of parachuting, I did not take that fear lightly. While I was waiting to jump, anticipation of the next few seconds had my full and undivided attention. I would not say that my mind was functioning in an alert, responsive manner; rather, I was moving on autopilot. I continued to do what I had practiced to the point of boredom. Though jumping from thirty-four feet or from a thousand feet might not be in my best interest, I would do it. But, it did not come easily.

Another big contributor to my fear was the waiting, both in the line winding up the stairway of the thirty-four-foot jump tower and in the C-123 aircraft for my first parachute jump. In both situations, it would have been easier for me if I could have been first out both doors, action with no time for thinking about it. Doing nothing allowed my brain to get a full workout. I entertained all of the what-ifs. I usually do not dwell on negative thoughts and instead push them to the back of my mind if I cannot discard them completely. But for some reason that tactic did not work for me during these two events; the pessimistic thoughts were there to stay. I felt fear, and I fed it with any and everything that entered my mind.

Personal pride, I suppose, made me jump from that door on the thirty-four-foot jump tower and the aircraft. True, good reasoning should have convinced me that I was not going to die while jumping, but at the time, I was not reasonable. In both cases, I could not have felt worse or had more fear if the hatchet man himself were standing by the door, blade raised. Nevertheless, I kept moving and I went out of those doors.

Normally, even in combat, I am fairly optimistic. But during the two events discussed here, I was very much a pessimist. I had a sense that I was not going to come out of these experiences well. The parachute issued to me for that first jump looked well used. The packing card showed that it had been used for eighty-seven jumps. Damn! My chances for survival would surely have been better with a new parachute.

It was not confidence in gear, equipment, instructors, or any outside thing that moved me toward those doors. My handling of those fears had to do with me, who I was and wanted to be, and the awareness that I would face the world tomorrow. While I surely did not think of it at the time, the bottom line was that I did not want anyone to be able to say, "Fox chickened out." That attitude has come close to getting me into real trouble several times in my life. But I suppose it fits under the word *adventure* and what we expect of ourselves.

Luck was on my side many times, and I do not hesitate to give it its' due. However, the courage that I felt during those difficult times came from my parents and the way I was reared. In addition, friends, associates, and the Marine Corps all had a hand in giving me that outlook on who I wanted to be, as a person and as a Marine.

I learned to love parachuting, and on those days years later when I made as many as ten jumps, I went through the routine as comfortably as I walked into my dining room for dinner with my family.

Riptide

MY PATHFINDER TEAM 44 from 1st Force Reconnaissance Company at Camp Pendleton, California, was on a thirteen-month temporary duty assignment to the 3rd Marine Division on Okinawa in 1962. One summer day (a day following a major storm on the island) we were scheduled to do rubber boat work and scuba diving off Onna Point, Okinawa. I was to be one of the first divers and made ready with my gear.

We were using Marine Corps Special Service diving gear; any qualified Marine who wanted to could use this equipment, so I had a certain lack of confidence in its quality. Leaking mouthpieces and facemasks as well as nonfunctioning air regulators were not unusual, so I decided to check out my gear before going out to sea. After telling my swim buddy of my intent, I entered a small pool of water beside a big rock on the water's edge right at the beach. As planned, I lay forward in the pool to completely submerge my system for the gear checkout.

Unbelievably, the next thing I knew, I was moving quickly out to sea. Sharp and dangerous, huge boulders of rough coral rock swept by me. I was fortunate to be in the center of the water channel and the channel was large enough to allow me to pass without brushing against that sharp coral. But those rocks took off their pound of flesh, and I lost enough as it was. My scuba gear was working, and I was extremely grateful for this. I was breathing air, and with the excitement of the situation, I was using plenty of it.

Fear came with the realization that I was in a riptide, a washout to sea over which I had no influence or control. If I could avoid contact with the rough coral reefs, being swept seaward and submerged underwater was not a concern as long as my scuba gear worked. I was breathing good air. I remembered reading somewhere that riptide forces slacken farther from shore, so I did not fight to rise to the surface; instead, I rode it out. I entertained a high anxiety level and my stress was no doubt measurable, but after the initial surprise, fear left me for the moment. Being underwater was not a problem.

The water force weakened and I rose to the surface to find that I was several hundred yards from the beach. Not a problem, I thought. I will swim in on the surface. Swimming, however, turned out to be a major problem. I was still in the stream of water headed seaward, and I was not making any headway with strong swim-fin strokes. In addition, the waves were so rough that I was underwater most of the time. I was still breathing from my scuba gear, so as long as the air held, I was all right. But the Special Services scuba tank was small with a limited air capacity. Thoughts of my air supply registered loudly and clearly, and I started conserving air by breathing about one breath in a normal requirement of three. Nevertheless, my hard flutter kicks were burning up air. When I realized that getting safely ashore was not going to be easy, I became alarmed.

The major cause of my fear was my lack of control over what was happening to me. I was on the surface yet underwater half of the time. Would my air hold out? Now on the surface and in spite of great physical effort, I clearly had negative progress in moving toward the beach and safety. I was going nowhere.

My fear was fed with the realization that I could not swim in against the outbound current. To my right on the beach was a big flat rock extending into the water. I had to get out of this riptide; I would head for that rock. The flanking action worked, and I made headway for a change. I continued to control my use of air; I took a breath when I had to have it. The waves continued to be so rough that, although I was swimming on the surface, I was underwater more than half of the time. My movement toward the rock was encouraging; I would make it. However, my arrival at the rock would feed my earlier fear by bringing on a new concern.

My getting on the rock turned out to be difficult. Each time I swam and crawled onto it, the strong returning waves washed me back into the ocean. I was washed off the rock with the returning water, and worse, my bare head was battered by the scuba tank loosely strapped on my back as I was tossed around the rock by the waves. I knew that the metal tank and the heavy wave action could and would do grave damage to my head if I continued to swim on and wash off the rock. Yet, I hesitated to part with that ready source of good air. Crawl on, wash off; the worsening situation fed my fear.

In the end, action and activity helped me handle my fear. I had experienced several different fears as I was caught in the riptide: (1) I realized I was in a washout to sea; (2) I could be chewed up by the rough coral reefs; (3) I wondered whether my air would last as long as I needed it; and (4) I wondered if I would ever make it to shore. I was on the shoreline, but I was roughly washed seaward off the rock each time I tried to recover ashore. I realized that I had to do something with my scuba tank because it would likely cause a head injury—my head hurt!

At this point I was at a loss concerning what to do next, as well as exhausted from the efforts put forth in my fight shoreward. I needed and received help. My fellow Pathfinders moved onto the huge bolder and, with the use of ropes, extended themselves in a human chain down to where I was being severely battered. They pulled me ashore and all was well. My team saved me.

10

Parachute Jumps

I REALLY ENJOYED JUMPING from an aircraft in flight, but there were ups and downs in my comfort level with parachuting. I left Force Reconnaissance in late 1962 with fifty-nine total military jumps, including nine free falls. My next assignment was to the Marine Aviation Detachment at the Naval Air Station in Jacksonville, Florida, where I learned that the air station had an active sport parachute club. I had become comfortable enough with parachuting that I decided to continue to do it for fun.

Parachuting was part of my life for the next twenty-three years, while I was in reconnaissance units; while I was in the Marine Corps Combat Development Center, Quantico, Virginia, as the reconnaissance officer; and, of course, while I continued parachuting for sport. The Development Center assignment involved evaluating new parachute designs and different methods of parachute entry into an objective area. All aspects of parachuting became more routine for me, and I handled them as easily as my deskwork in the office.

My duties as a jumpmaster (a person responsible for safe parachuting who, among other tasks, checks individual jumper equipment on the ground, monitors conduct in the aircraft, and releases jumpers at the place that will get them safely on the drop zone below, in both military and sport parachuting) and involvement with other jumpers' equipment checks allowed little time for thoughts of myself. On a number of occasions outside the aircraft door, as I spread into a good free-fall arch, I wondered if I had hooked my leg straps. The jumpmaster's work in the aircraft requires a lot of moving around. Usually I would unhook my leg straps rather than endure the discomfort, if not pain, of the leg straps' squeeze on my pelvis and lower torso. I would hook these straps back up as the plane made its approach for my stick's exit, for which I was often also the jumpmaster.

I always hooked the leg straps, but out in a full arch, I could not always feel the pressure of them on my body, causing me to wonder, "Did I hook them this time?" I would move a hand down to make sure. The cost of this doubt was usually a small loss of the flat and stable free-fall body position, a small price to pay for the acquired peace of mind.

Over my jump years, I accumulated 1,198 parachute jumps of which seven required me to activate my reserve (emergency) parachute to land on the ground safely. Here I will address three of these reserve activations as they caused me fear. The other four happened so fast and I remedied the situation so quickly that the threat was over before I had time to think or worry about it. Of course, good training was also a factor here. I will also discuss two other jumps that didn't involve my parachute canopy. In these cases, had I not taken the correct action, my contact with the ground would have been my end. In both of these jumps, I had plenty of time to become aware of the fear building up in me.

A Jump in High Wind

My fifth sport jump at Whitehouse Field near Jacksonville in

1963 was one of the two not involving a canopy malfunction. This jump took place on a windy, bright sunny day, and of course, the strong wind concerned the club leadership. Our wind meter indicated that the gusts were not over fifteen miles per hour, the maximum wind speed considered safe for parachuting. The club safety officer determined that only the experienced jumpers would be allowed to jump until the wind died down. Though I was new to the sport, my Marine jumps counted as experience and I was allowed to go. However, my personal parachute (a modified aviator's twenty-eight-foot survival canopy) was not effective against strong wind.

In those days, sport parachutists all bought and used surplus military canopies that were modified to provide a steering capability and a forward drive. My problem was that my chute had the least material cut out of it, a design known as a "double L." This modification gave me softer landings but less forward drive. Other parachutists had their chutes modified with what was known as a "TU," more canopy material cut out giving more forward drive. Because of my parachute, I should have remained on the ground, but I did not. My canopy's weakness in drive did not even enter my mind.

The jumpmaster tapped me out at 3,600 feet over the exit point. I was the first out and jumped alone. After a ten-second free fall, I deployed my chute. Under my open canopy, I realized that I was moving quickly over the drop zone, which included a concrete runway. The wind now at my jump altitude surely was different from what we had measured earlier on the ground. In fact, right after I jumped out of the plane, the jumpmaster received a radio message: "Not clear to jump—unsafe winds." A parachutist was on the ground serving as drop zone control, and he was responsible for the wind meter readings. He was on the radio with our pilot who relayed the word to the jumpmaster back in the plane during the jump run. Drop zone control was reading thirty-mile-per-hour gusts on his wind meter. The new reading came too late to benefit me; I was out, and my chute was open in it.

The runway lay in the wind's direction, and for a while I moved directly down the center of it. A landing on concrete at the speed I was moving would break me up, if it did not kill me, especially given my canopy's lack of forward drive. Parachutists jumping a canopy with good forward drive can face into the wind and reduce the wind's speed effect with the forward speed, or drive, of their parachute. My "double L"-modified military surplus parachute had maybe a two- to three-mile-per-hour drive, which was no help in wind gusts of twenty to thirty miles per hour. I did turn to the side, however, and managed to get off the path of the runway.

The causes of my fear were the strong wind and the realization of the consequences waiting for me upon landing. The terrain features flying by below me evidenced the wind strength and speed and the danger I now faced. Although drop zone control could communicate with the pilot, he could not talk with me once I was in the air. I was hanging up there by myself, learning as I moved through the air. The fast movement of the objects on the ground fed my fear.

I faced into the wind for the little benefit my canopy would give me. At 300 feet altitude, I watched my fast backward movement over the ground below. I was backing up at about twenty to twenty-five miles per hour and was concerned. I knew of Marines who had been killed jumping in high-wind —three on one jump with 1st Force Reconnaissance Company at Camp Pendleton, California.

I remember thinking at about twenty feet off the ground, "I have to do a good PLF [parachute landing fall] and go through all of my five points of contact (balls of the feet, side of lower leg, thigh, hip, and push-up muscle [side of chest]) upon hitting the ground." Backward PLF points of contact tend to be feet, butt, and head if the parachutist does not concentrate. Those three points of contact would be lethal in this wind. Thinking about my PLF is the last thing I remember about that jump.

I regained consciousness in a Jacksonville Naval Hospital bed with Dotti Lu looking into my face with great concern. She had been on the drop zone to watch our jump, and she knew that I was the first and only jumper out. She watched as I smashed into the ground with a backward parachute landing fall. The wind in my inflated canopy kept me moving on the ground until I hit a fence post with my head. Contact with either the ground or the fence post resulted in a concussion, and it took a month for me to get over double vision.

On this jump, my fear was caused by the knowledge that a parachute landing in that kind of wind speed hurts and can even kill you. Parachutists have been knocked unconscious upon ground contact and then dragged to their deaths by their wind-filled parachutes.

Parachute jumping after an injury from a prior jump is never an easy endeavor. While I waited for my eyesight to improve after the concussion, I continued with parachute club activities in any way a "grounded" jumper can, primarily serving as drop zone control. Finally, my doctor told me, "You're clear to jump, you dummy." I experienced concern and apprehension as each jump day (usually a Saturday) approached. However, for a month after my clearance to jump, the club had no naval aircraft support; there were either no pilots or no planes available. The longer I waited, the more concerned I became thinking about my next jump.

Our parachute club worked out a deal with the Jax Navy Flying Club: We would buy the gas if the club provided us with a plane and a pilot wanting the flight time. We were back in the air on the following Saturday. I not only had to wrestle with a jump following an injury, but that jump would be out of a strange aircraft, a Cessna 170. That combination certainly fed my fear about the coming jump.

While the effects of my concussion had faded, my concern about my next jump had not. Saturday arrived, and I showed up at the flying club for some training on jumping out of the smaller plane. What bothered me with this plane was the fact that the jumper had to crawl out the little open door and stand on the step while reaching out and taking hold of the strut under the overhead wing. The jumper was to hold on until the jumpmaster's signal to push off. This was more complicated than jumping out an open door.

The flight from the airport to the drop zone gave me much time for thought. And, of course, all of my thoughts centered around what could go wrong: the what-ifs. We passed over the drop zone, and the jumpmaster dropped the wind-drift indicator. The wind was light, and he gave me a thumbs-up question. I responded with a thumbs-up "ready" and displayed more spirit than I felt. This jump was not in my best interest; I did not want to do it.

On the jump run, the jumpmaster indicated for me to move into the door and out on the step. This movement helped. Full confidence returned as I hung on the strut and watched the ground move under me. Instead of fear, I felt a lift in spirit as I hung on outside of the aircraft. The rush of air around my body felt great as I studied the ground below me. With the signal, I pushed off into one of the easiest plane exits I have ever made, a slow fall away in a full-spread body position. My sport parachuting experience was on an upswing from then on.

No Parachute Out

The first of my three near-terminal parachute canopy mal-functions and my fourth reserve activation occurred when the parachute failed to come off my back after pulling my rip cord. This was jump number 531, and it took place on February 8, 1972, with the Quantico Sport Parachute Club. I was 2,500 feet from the ground when I pulled the rip cord, and in the slow-fall position of full spread, I was closing that distance at a speed in excess of 150 feet per second. A parachutist normally feels the chute come off his back and almost instantly begins the swing under it as the chute fills with air.

When I didn't feel the chute deploy, I looked over my shoulder to determine the problem, saw no canopy coming off my back, and immediately pulled my reserve rip cord positioned on my stomach. The canopy deployed with an opening shock (our reserve parachute canopies had no delayed-opening device in those days), and I was sitting in the saddle. All was well except that the main canopy fell from my backpack container with the opening shock.

Looking down, I saw that the sleeve (the delayed-opening device) of my main parachute was still around the canopy, preventing it from collecting air and inflating. Rather than pull my Capewell releases, cut away that canopy, and pull it out of the trees below, I decided to let it hang. I focused on the drop zone, which was far enough away that I might not make it out of the woods because of the fast rate of descent of my small reserve canopy.

I quickly learned that my reserve canopy had an auto-matic turn in it; I had to keep both hands on the steering toggles to continue straight ahead for the drop zone. At this point, I was relatively at ease as everything had happened so quickly. I was comfortable with the action I had just gone through. And, of course, my immediate reaction to the situation did not allow time for thoughts of fear.

Shortly, I noticed that the wind was causing the pilot chute to pull the sleeve off the main canopy hanging below me (naturally, that is the purpose of the pilot chute). The main parachute had to go; I had to cut it away. However, each time I released a steering toggle to pull my Capewell releases, my reserve canopy would start a fast turn to the rear. I was getting low and had to continue forward to clear the woods below. Stress was coming aboard and I recognized fear. What was I going to do?

An unfamiliar and apparently helpless situation was upon me. Because I had time to think about the situation, I realized my main canopy could inflate and rise to wrap around my reserve. The automatic turn in my reserve canopy left me with two choices: I could release the main canopy and suffer a tree landing with my small reserve parachute, which had no quick canopy releases to allow me to easily disengage from a tree. Or I could continue heading for the drop zone and accept that the main canopy could collect air and rise up to tangle with, and maybe wrap up, my reserve canopy, which could cause me to fall out of the sky. I chose to continue on toward the drop zone as it was now close by.

Feeding my fear was the strong possibility that my main canopy would clear the sleeve and inflate before I reached the ground. My anxiety rose as I watched the sleeve continue to slide down the canopy while the exposed part of the canopy was filling with air and helping to push the sleeve off. Maybe I would not make it; should I cut it away regardless of the circumstances? As I considered these thoughts, I realized that I was entering the drop zone. If the sleeve did not clear the canopy and if the chute did not fill with air, I should make it safely to the ground.

I continued toward the center of the drop zone because I had the air space before ground contact. Thinking back on the situation, I realize that once I was over the drop zone, I should have released my main canopy even though my reserve canopy would turn around. There were no trees to snag or entangle my canopy, and a landing anywhere on the field was satisfactory. My biggest concern should have been getting rid of the threatening main parachute. However, the thought never entered my mind. Frankly, I did not handle this fearful situation properly and in a safe manner. I should have dropped the main chute following the good opening of my reserve and later pulled that chute out of the trees.

Before I landed, my main canopy completely inflated, barber-poled up, and surrounded my reserve canopy. Fortunately for my family and me, I hit the ground just as my reserve parachute lost its lift ability. All was well. I would never again let a main canopy hang below me.

A Cut-Away with a Floating Reserve Parachute

My third high-stress, frightful jump and second bad canopy malfunction came on August 19, 1977, a Marine Corps parachute operation and my 655th jump. I was the cause of my troubles on this jump. I had just started jumping with the Strata Cloud, a new high-glide, low-descent-rate parachute known as a "square," which we were evaluating for Force Reconnaissance use. There was a lot of talk among jumpers about "end cell closures" on this particular popular parachute canopy. A friend asked me if I had experienced the problem on my last sport jump. Not having seen an end cell closure, I was not sure what he was talking about, so I said, I didn't think so; I had had an easy, comfortable landing.

For my next military jump on Friday of the following week, I elected to jump alone, open my chute at a high altitude, and play with it to get to know it. After a free fall from 10,000 feet, I opened my chute at 4,000 feet. Sitting in the saddle, I checked my canopy and it looked good to me.

Orientating on the drop zone, which was a long way off (as planned because of my high opening altitude and the wind speed that day), I decided to get comfortable. Normally one cannot see one's feet while hanging in the harness because the chest-mounted reserve parachute blocks the downward view. Rather than looking over my reserve parachute to see the ground, I decided to unhook one end. Releasing my bellyband and the left main lift web snap hook, I let the reserve hang down on my right side. I had a clear view of anywhere I might land. Then I played with and studied my main canopy.

Shortly, I knew what end cell closures looked like. I had them. The flying surface of the canopy was made up of nine cells that allowed air to flow through them, front to rear, as the parachutist descends. The cell on each side did not always inflate upon opening. This reduced the glide ratio a bit, but not enough to cause great alarm, especially considering that I was unaware I had end cell closures on the earlier jump. The solution to end cell closures is to pull half brakes to force the end cells to inflate. I had a somewhat casual attitude toward the end cell closures in part because a parachutist applies brakes upon landing and the cells inflate at that time, when lift is most needed.

I pulled half brakes and watched as the end cells inflated. Good! That is the way the chute was suppose to respond. However, my next act was not by the book. In my training, no one had mentioned what action should follow pulling half brakes, but I assumed that I was to let them off. Instead of releasing the brakes gradually or slowly, I let go of my turn toggles abruptly.

Immediately, I was in a fast, tight spin downward with two cells closed on one side. Bad news! After pulling half brakes again, my canopy straightened up and I was flying correctly. I released the toggles again only to go into the same tight downward spiral to the opposite side with two cells on that side closed. My stress level increased. I began to feel fear. What was happening? What was the matter with this parachute? It never dawned on me to release the brakes slowly. Once more, I pulled half brakes, forcing the canopy to fly correctly. Again, I released the toggles, and again, I went into a hard, fast downward spiral. I had had enough of this mad spiraling stuff. To hell with end cell closures; the ground was coming up to meet me!

I had opened my parachute at a high altitude, but I had no idea how far the spirals had lowered me. I decided that before I sunk any lower, I would cut away from the uncontrollable canopy. Although I was unable to read my altimeter in the fast, hard spin, I thought I was high enough for a cut-away and deployment of my reserve parachute. I pulled both canopy releases and was back in free fall, in a back-to-earth position coming out of the spin.

My cut-away from the square parachute was a standard procedure that I had performed several times previously. Nevertheless, I experienced fear caused by several sources: the biggest source of my fear was the fact that I had only one parachute left to get me safely to the ground. Another factor was the unknown: What else could happen that I would not be prepared for? My fear of an unknown situation was followed immediately with a huge shock of fright. As I fell in that back-to-earth position, facing skyward, my chest-mounted reserve parachute rose up over me. One retainer hook on the right side of the parachute pack was attached to my harness main lift web D-ring and the other end rose straight up in the air over me. What a feeling of fear, loss, and stupidity! I had released that end of my reserve parachute earlier to get a better view of the ground beneath me.

Fear seldom comes in more explosive packages than this. I consciously reminded myself that I had to remain cool, to do the right things. I had only one chance to perform the correct recovery procedure.

As I fell on my back toward the ground and attempted to hook the reserve parachute snap, my mind continued to move through the facts facing me at that instant. I remembered the instruction in jump school that one can land safely with only one reserve parachute snap hook attached to one main lift web D-ring. However, that type of hookup would be an uncontrollable mess with my steerable reserve parachute. I would be hanging cockeyed from the canopy by one set of risers while the other set of risers and the left steering toggle would be too far up to reach. I did not want to experience that.

My situation demanded that I handle this fear well if I wanted to continue to live on our great earth; I pushed fear aside. I would handle this like I learned close order drill: by the numbers. I reasoned, "I have plenty of altitude but none to play with. I will make one attempt to hook the left side of my reserve, and whether it hooks or not, I'll pull the reserve parachute ripcord. The reserve parachute should lower me safely to the ground with just one side hooked to the main lift web D-ring."

Grabbing the reserve pack, I pulled it down and positioned it across my stomach while also slowly and deliberately pulling it upward toward my chin. I felt the click as the snap link closed on the D-ring, and I pulled the rip cord. My little reserve parachute canopy opened properly and promptly. I had a third chance on life, and the awareness of that fact was strong within me.

I oriented on our drop zone, which was now too far away because of the long exit point for the higher opening, the altitude lost in the spin and cut-away, and the smaller reserve canopy that was now over me. At first I thought I'd make a tree landing in the woods, I was able to avoid the trees and land in a small clearing. I had a long walk through the woods to our drop zone, but I was enjoying life; I had no complaints.

Free Fall in a Flat Spin

Quantico Marine parachute operations were conducted on Fridays and sport parachuting took place on Saturdays. My 660th sport parachute jump on August 20, 1977 (the day following the jump just discussed), forced me to think about whether or not I would be around much longer. (Having a bad jump two days in succession could well cause an intelligent person to give it up.) And, like my sport jump in high wind, this one did not involve malfunction of the parachute canopy. Our Quantico Sport Parachute Club had another beautiful jump day—warm, sunshine, and no wind. The drop zone was loaded with parachutists wanting to add numbers to their jump log.

Four of us were on a UH-1E helicopter going to 10,000 feet. Our plan was to exit the aircraft with two jumpers leaping from each side of the aircraft on the word, "Go." We would get together quickly with a four-man hookup and play with it from there downward.

In a full-body spread outside of the aircraft, I reasoned that we would indeed do a quick hookup. As the pin man, I was about to turn and close on the base man (we were to be the first connected with the other two jumpers joining us). I did a hard-body turn to my left and instantly received a hit against my foot, in the same direction of my turn, from the parachutist who exited with me on my side of the aircraft.

Immediately I was in a flat spin. I could not focus on anything, and all I could see was a bright blur of light. I did not consider the foot strike as a source of my problem. I thought I was caught in a whirlwind even though there had been no wind on the ground. Where had the flat spin come from? Where and what was happening to my fellow jumpers? In my previous 659 parachute jumps, I had not experienced anything like this. If it were a whirlwind (which was never addressed in training), I would use what I was taught to get out of a flat spin: "Pull your arms and legs into a good tight airborne tuck and you will fall out of the spin."

I tried to tuck and found it next to impossible to pull in my arms, let alone my legs, because of the great centrifugal force caused by the spin. I became concerned, really concerned. Stressful thoughts rushed through my mind: How do I get out of this situation when what I have been taught does not work? I could not focus on a thing, and I lost all track of time. What was happening? Fear was with me and I knew it. I recognized fear and its cause.

Thinking about falling into a whirlwind is bad enough; believing that I was caught in the powerful grips of one gained my instant, close attention. Initially, my anxiety level was high because I had never been in this situation before. And as the seconds passed, I grew more afraid with the realization that I was having difficulty pulling in my arms and legs.

The blurring flat spin continued; the ground was coming up to me at a speed greater than 170 feet per second (the fast drop speed of a body falling through the air). I strained hard to draw in my arms and legs while fear of what might well happen filled my thoughts. The fear caused by the unexpected and the uncertainty of the situation was made worse by my inability to react or respond. And because I could not physically do anything but try to pull in my limbs, I had time to think and thereby feed my fear. I finally was able to get my arms to my side and my legs pulled up, but the spin continued. All of this time I was thinking: What is happening? How low am I? How long have I been falling? What else can I do to get out of this spin?

I considered pulling the rip cord to open my parachute. The parachute would be a tightly twisted mess if it opened at all; however, it would give me a better chance of survival than would hitting the ground without any reduction in my falling speed. If the twisted mess got me out of the spin before ground contact, I could cut it away and activate my reserve parachute—if I had the air space left. One thought followed another, all feeding my fear.

I thought I was in a whirlwind because I could not get out of the spin with the action I had been taught, and in all of my jumping experience, I had never been in a flat spin. There was not much I could do to handle the fear building up inside of me. When would the whirlwind play out, move off, and let go of me? The only thing I could do after I withdrew my arms and legs was hold that airborne tuck tightly. My mind continued to race with negative thoughts. How far have I fallen and how close am I to the ground?

Finally, my spin stopped. I was falling in a back-to-earth position and in a good airborne tuck. The bright blur before my eyes became the sun. I went into a free-fall spread-eagle, pulled in one arm in order to roll over for a belly-down position, and checked my altimeter. I had plenty of altitude! My altimeter read 6,000 feet; my spin had used up 4,000 feet. Maintaining a full spread eagle to ensure the slowest fall rate, I continued down to 2,500 feet. I made no turns or any other maneuvers; I wanted to enjoy this no-stress fall.

I learned later that I had not been caught in a whirl-wind. My jump buddy apologized for hitting my foot as I started the tight turn in the same direction, and I realized the hit had put me in a flat spin. I have no idea how I ended up on my back or when I turned over. Flat spins, as I learned after over 600 jumps, are not easy to recover from.

Double Parachute Malfunction

A double malfunction is the dread of all parachutists. It is the malfunction of both the main and the reserve canopies. Because this occurrence is rare, most parachutists think it never happens; they think double malfunctions are just a rumor, something to talk about, a subject that catches everyone's ear. In my twenty-three years of parachuting, I know of and was involved in two—one of them my own.

The first double I experienced happened during a Saturday jump with the Quantico Sport Parachute Club at Quantico, Virginia. We had a crystal clear sky, with shirt-sleeve temperatures, and no wind; we had planned to make many jumps. A Navy lieutenant commander and I jumped together on a pass of the aircraft over the drop zone. We planned to do relative work (join together) during free fall, and he was going to open his chute at 4,000 feet. He was jumping a new square chute that he had just purchased, and he wanted to play with it, to learn how to fly it, without having to suffer the consequence of hard ground contact if he messed up lower down.

We did our free fall, and I saw him open his chute high as planned. I continued down to 2,500 feet and deployed my chute. As I swung in the saddle during the opening shock, I was surprised to see a body falling by me. I wondered how the aircraft had gotten around so quickly on another jump run and how those parachutists had caught me in free fall.

Also, I was at the minimum safe-opening altitude. I thought, "You had better pull your rip cord, buddy!"

Then I realized that the falling body had to be that of the commander. For whatever reason, he had cut away from his main parachute (perhaps he experienced something similar to my cut-away situation described previously). Back in free fall, he had deployed his new back-mounted reserve parachute. The canopy had come out of his pack tray and snagged on his metal Capewell releases. He had opened these Capewells to release his main canopy, and they remained open as grappling hooks. He fell by me in a sitting position and pulled on his canopy with both hands, trying to free it from the release. He never freed the reserve chute, and I busied myself with checking my canopy as I did not want to watch him hit the ground. In respect to the commander, his wife, and three daughters, we secured our jumping on that otherwise beautiful day.

Several hundred jumps later, I experienced my own double malfunction during a Marine Reconnaissance Parachute Operation at Quantico, Virginia. On June 2, 1978, not only did I experience a malfunction with both my main and reserve canopies, but I also learned after my reserve chute opened that this reserve canopy had two malfunctions. Thus jump number 797 involved my worst parachute malfunction. It also rates right at the top with the extreme emotions it evoked: stress, concern, and fear for life.

When I pulled my main parachute rip cord at opening altitude of 2,500 feet, a blob of stuff trailed me at the end of my parachute suspension lines. Somehow, the slider, whose purpose is to slow the canopy opening, was entangled with the canopy, creating a ball of stuff that had little chance of inflating before ground contact. I pulled my canopy releases, which put me back in free fall and on my back.

Releasing my main parachute because of a canopy malfunction was standard procedure, so Old Man Fear did not make an appearance up to this point. My difficulties began when I did not use up any more altitude by rolling over on my stomach. I should have rolled over because I had a back-mounted reserve parachute. Truthfully, in the rush of the moment, I had forgotten I had a back-mounted reserve. This type of reserve parachute was new to me, as all of my earlier reserve parachute activation experiences, including those in training, had been with chest-mounted reserves. I pulled the reserve parachute rip cord.

The back-mounted reserve canopy moved around my falling body and opened above me with one major problem. My suspension lines were twisted from my shoulders to the canopy skirt. The line twist was so tight that I could not get my head back through the lines in order to look up and check my canopy. My head was held forward and down because of the line pressure. Finally, by twisting sideways and working around the rope of suspension lines, I was able to look upward.

The line twist to the canopy skirt had greatly reduced the lift area of the canopy by drawing the skirt inward and together. I was dropping faster than I expected, and I noticed that I had one or more suspension lines over the canopy causing what is known as a "Mae West." This malfunction makes two smaller canopies out of the single larger one and causes a much faster rate of descent. As I assessed my parachute's condition my stress level rose; I was aware that major injury or death could be upon me within the next minute.

Fear was knocking heavily on my mental door. I realized that I probably would not survive contact with the ground under this small chute modified as it was with two suspension line problems. I had to correct at least one, and preferably both of the malfunctions, and quickly.

The strong possibility of major injury or death was the cause of my fear. Unless immediate corrective action was taken on that reserve canopy so that it functioned with a safe lift capability, I was going to be, at the least, seriously hurt. At the rate I was descending, I had less than sixty seconds to make the corrections.

Yet, there was time for my fear to be fed and grow. Considering the amount of material a mind can work with in one second, I had plenty on hand to work over. After I determined that I had a Mae West in addition to the bad line twist, I had many seconds for thought. Only the ground that was quickly coming up toward me limited the feeding of my fear. Maybe I would not hit the ground hard enough to kill myself, but even broken bones were unacceptable. I reasoned that I must make a perfect parachute landing fall by hitting all five points of contact.

Looking downward, I saw that I would land in the forest. With a little luck, maybe I would fall through a tree, with limbs that could catch my chute before I hit the ground.

I handled my fear in this situation in much the same way as I had during my earlier experiences—with action. The cut-away of my malfunctioned main parachute handled my original concern quickly enough. The determination that my reserve parachute had bad line twists as well as a Mae West now provided a major fear, especially when I noted my fast rate of descent. After I diagnosed the malfunctions, there was time to consider my bad situation and the limited means available to me to rectify it. Once again my thoughts included: keep a cool mind, do not rush through any action, and react by the numbers, one thing at a time.

The Mae West threatened my safe landing the most. With that malfunction, the parachutist usually attempts to pull on the riser with the suspension lines that are over the canopy, causing them to slide off. The line or lines slide off and all is well, provided there are no major friction burns on the canopy material from the nylon-on-nylon movement over it.

I could do nothing about the Mae West until I had my lines untwisted. My focus and effort had to be on one problem at a time, and my first job was to untwist my lines. Then, if I had the time before ground contact, I would work on the Mae West.

I began kicking my legs and working my arms to increase my spinning under the canopy. There was a natural untwisting taking place, but it was not fast enough. I would be on the ground before the lines were free on their own. With vigorous action, I put myself in a fast spin, and I kept it going. Not only did this action make me dizzy, but it also made me feel sick. I could not focus on anything, but I kept the spin going.

There was a wide swing as the lines finally freed themselves, and then I started twisting up in the opposite direction because of the spin's momentum. I worked to counter the new spin. All spinning stopped, and I looked up to see what I could do about clearing the Mae West.

It was gone! It had worked itself out when the lines freed themselves from the twist. And, at that instant, I hit the ground. I was not prepared for a parachute landing fall body position—just feet, butt, and head. My focus had been on the canopy, not the approaching ground.

I was in the woods among small trees and fortunately had missed landing on one. I hurt all over and was greatly pleased to feel the pain—it meant that I was alive. As I moved my limbs I determined that I probably had not broken any major bones. In spite of the pain, I was extremely happy. The pain went slowly away. I would jump again.

Courage may have played some role in getting me into parachuting initially, but what really got me through these close calls was training and keeping a cool head or mind while carrying out what I had been taught to do in those situations. Yes, I was lucky as well. I noted when referring to my jump log to get the date on jump number 797 that jump number 798 followed on the same day and within a half an hour. Then the next day, Saturday, I made eight parachute jumps on the same drop zone with the Quantico Sport Parachute Club. Fall off the horse, get right back on!

11

Our Fearful World

THE WORDS *FEAR* AND *ENEMY* are closely related. If *enemy* means something or anything that will or could do us harm, then with an enemy we have one of the main causes of fear. All animals have enemies, from insects to humans. For example, the lion is an enemy of most animals, including man. But the lion's primary intent is not to harm others; it is merely his way of life to kill other mammals for food. In contrast, man causes fear in his fellow man not to survive, as with the lion, but to gain material benefits. Throughout the ages man has been, and no doubt will continue to be, the enemy of man.

This description of the enemy, those that would do harm to others, surely fits the part played by the terrorist organization al Qaeda. It is well-known that the people of al Qaeda have dedicated their lives to destroying certain people, their societies, and their ways of life. As long as the human race has existed there has been a group of people with this murderous mentality. There is much printed on the subject, including *Flyboys: A True Story of Courage* by James Bradley. Bradley writes about the Japanese government and military's brutal handling of the Chinese at the beginning of the twentieth century and of American aviator prisoners of war, to include eating their flesh, during World War II. The Japanese people were not terrorists; that was their leadership's mentality at the time and the manner in which they raised their young people.

Why do people commit acts of terrorism? What is the terrorists' purpose in killing people of all ages and both sexes? Of course, the answer is they kill people to instill fear and thereby get what they want. Their targets are people, and people, like flies, are everywhere. The goals of today's terrorists are somewhat achievable because they have an assistant and, in many ways, a major supporter—though I recognize that the support is not intentional. Who or what provides this support? The news media.

The fastest and most effective way for terrorists to deliver their message to the people, to all of the people, is to get news media coverage. And, of course, the bigger events—those with a large number of people killed and hurt—garner the most media coverage. Was there any media service anywhere in the world that did not cover the situation in New York City on September 11, 2001? That coverage did not last only one day but many weeks, and it continues today. Most of us were aware of a monumental feeling of fear on that day, and we recognize a threat yet today. The induction of fear on 9/11 cost the terrorists practically nothing in comparison to the damage and loss that it caused for others.

We suffer the fear induced by these terrorists' acts and the consequences of experiencing this fear all courtesy of one of our prized rights of freedom, our free press. Yes, the press can and will provide to us, the consumer, with anything that they feel will cause us to invest in their media product. It is our right to have access to this information, and we should know what is going on in our world. But, at what price? Are the 9/11 attacks and similar acts that may follow an acceptable price for this freedom?

I may be way off, but I think that these awful events would not happen if the terrorists knew that few, if any, people would learn about them. If only a few people learned about a tragedy, how could fear be provided and grow? I am not against the media service; their service is one we need. I just wish there were some way that the media served our citizens without benefiting the terrorist.

Our leadership needs to know what is happening in the world, and they have their own means and sources of information. Good positive leadership can and will handle issues that affect the good of the people. Such leadership can occur in spite of whether the people know about possible attacks in advance, and actions taken by good leadership will differ little if the citizens are warned of attacks in advance. We, the people, must ensure that we have the best and most capable people in positions of leadership. Then, maybe we can live with less media coverage and knowledge of the ugly terrorist acts, especially considering the terrorists' reliance on fear.

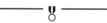

Who is the enemy? Who are these bad guys? I remember reading and hearing about the Six-Day War in 1967 and the little country of Israel fighting circles around their enemy who had a much larger force. These forces were no doubt poorly trained and equipped, but in size alone they should have made an accounting of themselves. I believe the problem among the Arab troops was the rank and file facing the Israelis felt that the effort was not worth their lives. There were also, of course, major problems with Arab leadership at all levels, both militarily and politically.

My thoughts are that those Arab forces performed so poorly that someone or a group of people decided to do something about it. He or it started to raise children with a mind-set that life on this earth is temporary and that people should move onward to the greater life following this one as soon as possible. The terrorist threat is not from a national force of considerable size and commanding presence; it is from individuals and groups who commit brutal acts to scare others into compliance with theirs or their mastermind's desires. While there is some national influence in the background, no nation has come forward with that commitment.

I suppose U.S. support of the Israelis in the 1967 war is a factor terrorists consider when they decide who to hurt, who to destroy, and where to cause and institute fear. America must be hurt. Americans must feel pain and fear for their very lives. I don't know enough about the national situations at the time to approach thoughts reference our country's political support for either the Arabs or the Israelis. But I do feel that therein lies the cause for today's terrorist acts against our country.

What was the mentality of those conducting the airplane flights that crashed into the World Trade Center, the Pentagon, and a Pennsylvania field? Did they feel either courage or fear? I don't think so. Those individuals were on automatic drive and were simply doing what had been instilled in them since childhood, to fulfill their purpose on earth. These young people, today's and tomorrow's terrorists, are raised with suicide as their life's mission. Of course, their mission of suicide includes taking others' lives with them. And underlying all of these evil acts against humanity are those wonderful promises of what the terrorists will earn in their next life. Upon hearing these promises, a sensible man should have thought that maybe all was not as presented. The children should have asked their teachers, "If the afterlife is so great, why aren't you taking advantage of this great opportunity?"

And where were the masterminds, the leaders who thought up, planned, and financed the inhuman, devilish, and horrific actions of September 11? They were surely not out there with their troops, leading from the front or from any other noticeable position. They were safely hidden underground in some backward country taking advantage of poor people, and there they will remain. Their goal could be stated as, "It is not our purpose to die for our country, our beliefs, or our desires, but to make good, caring, responsible people (and families) die for theirs." Why do these supposed "leaders" not rush into the next great life that offers so much, that is so much better than the one here on earth, the one they sell to their followers? Because they know better.

How long can this terrorist war last? Fortunately for us, members of the terrorists' rank and file are not of the George Patton mentality. I agree 100 percent with General Patton's statement to his soldiers, "It is not our purpose to die for our country, but to make the other poor son of a bitch die for his!" The terrorist dies for his beliefs, if not for his country, and sometimes he dies by his own hand. How many are in the terrorist rank and file? How many young minds have been negatively influenced by evil people with the power to do so?

Terrorist leadership such as al Qaeda has been active for many years now and it is known that they have a sizable following. The following is comprised of people with the same thoughts and feelings as you and I experience. Their brains work for them as ours do for us, and I feel that the rank-and-file terrorists will eventually get smart as to what is happening and how they are being used. Is the cause really worth my life? They will ask.

Will tomorrow's replacements for the hard-core individuals who have left this world in some explosion be as dedicated to the terrorists' cause. I think not. People all over the world are getting better education, learning more and leading a better life than people did forty years ago.

12

Summary of Courage

AMERICANS ARE BLESSED with the good life in a great country, both of which were provided for us by our forefathers' hard work, courage, and determination. We will continue to enjoy our way of life because our brothers and sisters are of the same stock as those who have preceded us. Individual courage is the common factor, and the American has more than enough of this trait to ensure a future with the good life as solid as has been our past. The American can be counted on to answer the call, and most do not wait for the call but move out on their own.

I agree with Willie Nelson's sentiments in "My Heroes Have Always Been Cowboys." I would add country boys, farm boys, city boys, and town boys to that statement. American boys have always come through for their country, and they always will. True, some individuals have, for different reasons, avoided their national security responsibility, but they are a small minority. They fit the mold of the "Don't ask me!" followers. They do not count—for much.

I served with great Americans during my time with the Marine Corps, but some of those who wore the uniform with me did not do so as their first choice. Yes, they chose the

Marine uniform, but the Selective Service draft prompted their
decision to join in the first place. These young Marines served
our flag well, but some did not measure up to the rank and
file of today's Marines. Every Marine today wanted to be in
the armed services and, more important, in the Corps. It is
his or her desire to serve as a U.S. Marine, and in wartime,
this is a big order.

During my presentations and visits with Marines, I've
noticed a clear difference. These men and women are 100
percent–motivated, gung-ho young people with their eyes
on the skyline, going for it with little wasted effort. One has
to be in their presence for only a short time to be aware of
this strength and spirit.

A statement from George Orwell aptly describes the
young people who wear our country's uniforms in service to
our national cause today. Mr. Orwell said, "We sleep safely in
our beds because rough men stand ready in the night to visit
violence on those who would do us harm." This statement
was made in reference to those wearing our military uniforms
in the past, and it surely fits the young Marines I work with
today. I am not alone, by far, in viewing today's Marines in a
positive manner.

A mother, "Cybil," supports my point in her posting to
the website http://myMarine.com. She writes,

> For all of those who have sons or daughters at
> boot camp let me pass on what I found. Let me
> give you a little background first. When my son
> left home he had no motivation, he was lazy,
> sloppy, no pride, no self-worth. This is the boy
> who got off the bus March 18th at Parris Island.
> The man I met on Thursday for Parents Day is

AWESOME! There is no way I can describe the difference. He looks different, he walks different, he talks different, and he has such a sense of bearing and pride that all I could do was look at him in awe! Oh yes, the training is hard, what he went through is unimaginable to anyone who has not been there. They are definitely taught to be warriors. Let me tell you the surprise of what else they taught. My son has better values, better morals, and better manners than anyone I know. It is so much more than Yes Sir, Yes Maam . . . so much more. He cares about how he looks, he cares about what he does, and it is not a boastful, bad ass thing. He is a true gentleman. I saw patience and calmness in him that I have never seen. I could never express my gratitude enough to the Marine Corps for what they have given my son. I know this; I have an 11-year-old Devil Pup still at home. When the time comes for his turn, if I had to, I would take him kicking and screaming all the way. Although, I'm sure that will not happen. The hero worship I see in my younger son's eyes for his Marine brother tells me I will have two Marines in the family, and I will be one very proud mother.

Much credit goes to this mother who contributed to her son's transformation because she provided the bedrock that the Marine Corps built upon. Her son had those basic values because of the manner in which she taught and reared him. She also gave him the freedom to make his own decisions, to take the lesser demanding route in his daily happenings, and to fit in with the "cool" crowd. The Marine Corps took that bedrock material, took away his freedom to do as he wanted, and demanded his integrity, loyalty, obedience, promptness, accountability, knowledge, and physical fitness. Parents of Marines are team members; they provide the makings of Marines. I enjoy being among parents at their children's graduation from boot camp and Officer Candidates School. I seldom miss an opportunity to attend a graduation if I am in the area.

Following are more great quotes that summarize what the word *courage* means to many of us. Great leaders have spoken words that helped others get through rough times. While a leader might not be directly involved with the difficulty at hand, his or her words can have the power to bring people together to accomplish the task. Positive words from others give us courage, help us handle our worst fears, give us reason to continue, and remind us that there is light ahead.

Marines are a wonderful source of this verbal support. In every one of our major fearful crises, there has been at least one Marine leader who had something positive to say about the situation. Our media seems to follow Marines around in hopes of picking up and passing on these gems of courage. Positive words from those who are involved in the worst of situations can help all people who hear them. While not all of these quotes are directly related to courage in combat and handling fear, they express the faith and the confidence of the speaker in the U.S. Marines' ability to accomplish the difficult task at hand. These quotes tell the story of courage handling fear.

Words from Marines in Combat

"Retreat, hell! We just got here!"

This exclamation is credited to Capt. Lloyd Williams of the 4th Marine Brigade in the Bois de Belleau battle during

World War I. A retreating French officer leading his unit to the rear had recommended to Captain Williams that he withdraw his Marines because the Germans were advancing. Captain Williams's response says it all: fear or no fear, we know our mission, we are here to do it, and we will do it. Those within earshot of the captain must have taken some relief of their fear, if they had any. Their path of coming action was quite clear. Marines stopped the German assault and moved forward themselves.

————

"Come on, you sons of bitches! Do you want to live forever?"

GySgt. Daniel "Dan" J. Daly is credited with saying these words as he left the trenches near Lucy-le-Bocage and led his unit in the 5th Marine's attack into Belleau Woods, France, on June 6, 1918, in World War I. Who wants to live forever in the misery of trench warfare? Daly's words reminded his Marines that death could come today or tomorrow, but, if successful, the attack could end the trench madness. It worked; the Marines came out of their positions of relative safety in the trenches and attacked successfully into the direct fire of the German machine guns. From this action came the Marine's nickname "Devil Dogs" as the German soldiers compared their attackes to canines.

————

"I have only two men out of my company and twenty out of some other company. We need support, but it is almost suicide to try to get it here as we are swept by machine-gun fire and a constant barrage is on us. I have no one on my left and only a few on my right. I will hold."

1st Lt. Clifton B. Cates's report on July 19, 1918, surely did not give his commander a warm and fuzzy feeling about tomorrow. But the Devil Dogs held on and won that battle in World War I. Clifton Cates was the Marine Corps Commandant when I joined the Corps in 1950. His description of that situation, and the fact that he lived to become commandant, is a reminder that courage will take one the distance (a little luck also helps).

———

"Casualties many; percentage of dead not known; combat efficiency: we are winning!"

This was Col. David M. Shoup's report to Maj. Gen. Julian C. Smith during World War II. Shoup, the commanding officer of the 2nd Marine Regiment, reported to his commander of the 2nd Marine Division following the second day of the battle on Tarawa, in the Gilbert Islands of the Pacific. Fear had to be in the hearts of all Marines involved in that battle, especially when they saw so many of their comrades cut down in the water even before reaching the beach. Nevertheless, they continued forward. Shoup's words did not reach them or help them directly, but they sum up the general attitude of all Marines going ashore and into that fight. The Japanese started it and the Marines were there to finish it.

———

"My only answer as to why the Marines get the toughest jobs is because the average Leatherneck is a much better fighter. He has far more guts, courage, and better officers. These boys out here have pride in the Marine Corps and will fight to the end no matter what the cost."

2nd Lt. Richard C. Kennard, Peleliu, World War II, is credited with this statement. No one is in a better position to recognize and know the warrior spirit than a Marine 2nd lieutenant in combat.

———

"We're not retreating! Hell! We're just attacking in a different direction!"

Maj. Gen. Oliver P. Smith, commander of the 1st Marine Division in the Yudam-ni, Chosin Reservoir, North Korea, made this statement. His division was surrounded by ten divisions of the Chinese People's Liberation Army in subzero temperatures. Gen. Douglas MacArthur had earlier wanted the Marines to attack north to the Yalu River, but it made better sense to General Smith and his Marines to attack in a direction that might provide a tomorrow. Our Marines changed their directions and seven of those Chinese divisions were destroyed in the process. What leadership! Purpose and courage played a major role throughout this endeavor, as did the shared optimism of many individuals. Fear had to be plentiful, but it was handled by all within the ranks of Marines.

———

"Don't you forget that you're 1st Marines! Not all the communists in hell can overrun you!"

"So they've got us surrounded—good! Now we can fire in any direction. Those bastards won't get away this time!"

These are two of Col. Lewis B. "Chesty" Puller's quotes, as any Marines can tell you. Puller led the 1st Marine Regiment, and he was with General Smith in the fight out of the Chosin Reservoir.

———

"You cannot exaggerate about the Marines. They are convinced to the point of arrogance that they are the most ferocious fighters on earth—and the amazing thing about it is that they are."

Father Kevin Keaney said this when he served as 1st Marine Division chaplain during the Korean War. Our Navy provides chaplains for Marines, and they quickly get to know the men of their unit.

———

"Being ready is not what matters. What matters is winning after you get there."

Lt. Gen. Victor H. Krulak, who made this statement during the Vietnam War, April 1965, was involved in three wars: World War II, Korea, and Vietnam.

———

"Courage is endurance for one moment more . . ."

An unknown Marine second lieutenant made this statement during the Vietnam War. Marine 2nd lieutenants are rifle platoon commanders who lead three rifle squads in firefights with the enemy. No one knows more about the workings of courage and what it does for the unit.

———

"Every Marine is, first and foremost, a rifleman. All other conditions are secondary."

Gen. Alford M. Gray, USMC, Commandant of the Marine Corps, 1987–91, said this. Yes, the Corps has technicians, but at any moment they may well find themselves at the cutting edge, in a rifle squad. And, they will do the job required of them as Marines.

———

"The Chief of Naval Operations would never be called a sailor. The General of the Army would never be called a soldier. The chief of staff of the Air Force would never be called an airman. The Commandant of the Marine Corps is damned proud to be called a Marine."

Gen. Charles Krulak, Commandant of the Marine Corps, 1995–99, reiterates my point that all Marines are members of the team and esprit de corps is what makes the difference.

———

"We are United States Marines, and for two and a quarter centuries we have defined the standards of courage, esprit, and military prowess."

Gen. James Jones, Commandant of the Marine Corps, 1999–2003, puts into a few words what I have attempted to convey in this work. Courage will take one the distance, whether it is on the battlefield or in hometown, USA. Courage provides the means to do what should be done or resist what should not be done.

———

"I love the Corps for those intangible possessions that cannot be issued: pride, honor, integrity, and being able to carry on the tradition for generations of warriors past."

Cpl. Jeff Sornij, USMC, stated it well for all Marines in a *Navy Times* article, November 1994.

———

"O Lord, we have long known that prayer should include confession. Therefore, on behalf of Marines, I confess their sins:

"Lord, they're just not in step with today's society;

"They are unreasonable in clinging to old-fashion ideas like patriotism, duty, honor, and country;

"They hold radical ideas believing that they are their brother's keeper and responsible for the Marines on their flanks;

"They have been seen standing when colors pass, singing the national anthem at ball games, and drinking toasts to fallen comrades;

"Not only that, they have been seen standing tall, taking charge, and wearing their hair unfashionable short;

"They have taken John Kennedy's words too seriously and are overly concerned with what they can do for their country instead of what this country can do for them;

"They take the Pledge of Allegiance to heart and believe that their oath is to be honored;

"Forgive them, Lord, for being stubborn men and women who hold fast to such old-fashioned values; after all, what more can you expect? They are Marines!

"O Lord our God, bless our misguided ideals, continue to raise up in this nation strong leaders and deliver us from "me first" managers and "don't ask me" followers. Be our honored guest this day. Let it be a day of laughter, good food, good drink, and the telling of tall tales and legends that occasionally exceed the truth. Watch over and keep safe those who wear this nation's uniform with special attention to their families everywhere."

Dr. Daniel W. Pollard, a physician in Colorado, made this confession in his speech at a gathering of veterans in the 1980s. During his service time, he was a corpsman with the 1st Battalion, 9th Marines in Vietnam. All Marines accept the fact that a Fleet Marine Force Navy corpsman is one of us; he even wears our uniform, but with his own rank insignia.

How Others View Marines

The following quotes are not by Marines and some may not comment directly on courage and fear; however, they do refer to U.S. Marines, the masters at handling fear with courage. These quotes help tell the story of what Marines are all about, how they see themselves, and what we as a nation can expect from the courageous men and women who wear the Marine green.

"The deadliest weapon in the world is a Marine and his rifle."

"Why in hell can't the Army do it if the Marines can? They are the same kind of men—why can't they be like Marines?"

Both of these quotes are attributed to Gen. John J. "Black Jack" Pershing, U.S. Army, and were said at separate times during World War I. The general obviously saw a warrior quality in Marines that was possibly lacking in some of his units.

———

"The raising of that flag on Suribachi means a Marine Corps for the next 500 years."

James Forrestal, Secretary of the Navy, made this observation during World War II, February 1945. The secretary was aboard ship off of Iwo Jima on February 23, 1945, and seemed to be impressed with what he saw the Marines doing on that Japanese-held island.

———

"I can never again see a United States Marine without experiencing a feeling of reverence."

Gen. Harold K. Johnson, U.S. Army, survived the Bataan Death March as a young officer in World War II. In the Korean War, he was a regimental commander of the 7th Infantry, and later the 5th Cavalry and 7th Cavalry of the 1st Cavalry Division. He was involved in the United Nations pursuit into North Korea and the following withdrawal action in November 1950. He also was involved with Marine units, and his statement implies that they impressed him.

———

"The more Marines I have around, the better I like it!"

"The American Marines have it [pride], and benefit from it. They are tough, cocky, sure of themselves and their buddies. They can fight and they know it."

These quotes were said at separate times and attributed to Gen. Mark Clark, U.S. Army, Korean War. As a senior commander in that war, he was in a position to know.

———

"I have just returned from visiting the Marines at the front, and there is not a finer fighting organization in the world."

"If I had one more division like this 1st Marine Division, I could win this war."

These two quotes are attributed to General of the Army,

Douglas MacArthur, U.S. Army, Korean War. He requested and received the 1st Marine Division, Reinforced. A second combat strength Marine Division was impossible from the ranks of the 68,000 personnel of the Marine Corps in 1950. President Truman was convinced that Marines would not be needed in the future "push-button" wars.

———

"The safest place in Korea was right behind a platoon of Marines! Lord! How they could fight!"

"The 1st Marine Division is the most efficient and courageous combat unit I have ever seen or heard of."

Maj. Gen. E. Frank Lowe, U.S. Army, made these statements during the Korean War, January 1952. President Truman did not like the U.S. Marine Corps and did not want to believe what he was hearing in reference to the conduct of the war. He reactivated his friend, General Lowe, out of retirement and sent him over to investigate the U.S. force's problems in fighting that war. (After all, America had just fought and won the world's largest war five years earlier.) The first quote is the bottom line of General Lowe's study of the total force and probably not what Truman wanted to hear. He also assured the president that the Marine Corps was everything it claimed as a force in readiness, with the addition of his second statement.

———

"Panic sweeps my men when they are facing the American Marines!"

A captured North Korean major in the Korean War, made this statement during his interrogation.

———

"Do not attack the 1st Marine Division. Leave the yellow legs alone. Strike the American Army."

This order was given to Communist troops in the Korean War and revealed to the U.S. Military by several prisoner of war. Shortly after the order came to light, the Marines were ordered to not wear their khaki leggings (from which came the term "yellow legs"), and U.S. Army soldiers begin wearing the Marine camouflaged cloth helmet cover. This had been strictly a Marine item of wear through World War II and up to this point in the Korean War. Anything to confuse the enemy.

———

"The man who will go where his colors go, without asking, who will fight a phantom foe in a jungle and mountain range, without counting, and who will suffer and die in the midst of incredible hardship, without complaint, is still what he has always been, from Imperial Rome to sceptered Britain to Democratic America. He is the stuff of which legions are made. His pride is his colors and his regiment, his training hard and thorough and coldly realistic, to fit him for what he must face, and his obedience is to his orders. As a legionnaire, he held the gates of civilization for the classical world. . . . Today he has been called United States Marine."

Lt. Col. T. R. Fehrenbach, U.S. Army, included this observation in his book *This Kind of War: The Classic Korean War History*. These are beautiful words written by one who knows how to use them.

———

"We have two companies of Marines running rampant all over the northern half of this island and three Army regiments pinned down in the southwestern corner, doing nothing! What the hell is going on?"

General John W. Vessey Jr., U.S. Army, chairman of the Joint Chiefs of Staff, said this in reference to the U.S. action on Grenada in 1983. His Army airborne units had a tougher fight before them, but they seemed hesitant and were slow to take it on.

———

"Some people spend an entire lifetime wondering if they made a difference in the world. But the Marines don't have that problem!"

Ronald Reagan, president of the United States, made this statement in 1985. President Reagan received my vote and the Marines received his.

———

"U.S. Marines are the most peculiar breed of human beings I have ever witnessed. They treat service as if it was some kind of cult, plastering their emblems on almost everything they own, making themselves look like insane fanatics with hair-cuts to ungentlemanly length, worshiping the Commandant almost as if he was a god, and making weird animal noises like a gang of savages. They'll fight like rabid dogs at the drop of a hat just for the sake of a little action, and are the cockiest sons of bitches I have ever known. Most have the foulest mouths and drink well beyond man's normal limits, but their high spirits and sense of brotherhood set them apart and, generally speaking, the United States Marines I've come in contact with are the most professional soldiers and the finest men and women I have ever had the pleasure to meet."

"There are only two kinds of people that understand Marines: Marines and the enemy. Everyone else has a second-hand opinion."

"All militaries harden their recruits, instill the basics, and bend young men to their will. But the Marine Corps provides its members with a secret weapon. It gives them the unique culture of pride that makes the Marines the world's premier warrior force. The Navy has its ships, the Air Force has its planes, the Army has its detailed doctrine, but "culture"—the values and assumptions that shape its members—is all the Marines have."

"They call this culture 'esprit de corps.'"

"Alone among the U.S. military services, the Marines have bestowed their name on the enlisted ranks. The Army has Army officers and soldiers, the Navy has naval officers and sailors, the Air Force has Air Force officers and airmen—but the Marines have only Marines."

"Once a Marine always a Marine."

Gen. William Thornson, U.S. Army, made all of these statements. General Thornson obviously not only respected Marines as warriors, but liked them as well.

"Marines I see as two breeds, Rottweilers and Dobermans, because Marines come in two varieties, big and mean, or skinny and mean. They're aggressive on the attack and tenacious on defense. They've got really short hair and they always go for the throat."

R. Adm. Jay R. Stark, U.S. Navy, said this in November 1995 during his speech at a Marine Ball in which he likened members of each service to a particular breed of dog.

―――――

"I never knew many Marines who were only a 'little' dangerous. Most of them seem to be a 'lot' dangerous. That, I think, is the idea."

Toby Hughes was an Air Force fighter pilot during the Vietnam War. This was his written response to Assistant Secretary of the Army Sara Lister for her remark, "Marines are extremists and a little bit dangerous." Lister was fired from her post for her remarks.

―――――

"They told us to open up the U.S. Embassy or we'll blow you away. Then they looked up and saw Marines on the roof with those really big guns and they said in Somali, 'Igaralli ahow,' which means 'Excuse me, I didn't mean it, my mistake.'"

Karen Aquilar, U.S. Embassy, Mogadishu, Somalia, said this in 1991. Our State Department is involved with our Marines.

―――――

"I can't say enough about the two Marine Divisions. If I use words like 'brilliant' it would really be an under description of the absolutely superb job that they did in breaching the so called impenetrable barrier. It was a classic—absolutely classic—military breaching of a very very tough minefield, barbwire, fire trenches-type barrier."

Gen. Norman Schwarzkopf, U.S. Army Commander, Operation Desert Storm, said this in February 1991. The Marines were in Kuwait, and their action ended the war just as it started. General Schwarzkopf gives them their due.

———

This last quote is for all Americans who have answered the call for uniformed service to our great country during its time of need. Theodore Roosevelt states my sentiments well:

> It is not the critic who counts, nor the man who points out how the strong man stumbles, or where the doer of deeds could have done better. The credit belongs to the man who is actually in the arena; whose face is marred with dust and sweat; who strives valiantly; who errs and may fail again, because there is no effort without error or short-comings, but who does actually strive to do the deeds; who does know the great enthusiasm, the great devotion; who spends himself in a worthy cause: who at best, knows in the end the triumph of high achievement, and who at worst, if he fails, at least fails while daring greatly, so that his place shall never be with those cold and timid souls who know neither victory nor defeat.

I salute all soldiers, sailors, airmen, and Marines; their individual and team courage enables each of us to live the life we choose. They will always be there in force, as a team, to ensure that we have the freedom of personal choice, our way of life. Thank God and the mothers of all young Americans who ask and follow through with the answer to the question, "What can I do for my country?"

Index

About the Author

COL. WESLEY LEE FOX, USMC (RET), was an active duty Marine for forty-three years. He joined the Marines in 1950 for the Korean War and a four-year enlistment. In spite of his life goal of farming, he fell in love with the Marine Corps. He served two tours in Vietnam, his second war, and remarks that he really planned on making a career out of the Corps, but had to quit with only forty-three years after he hit the mandatory retirement age of sixty-two. However, he continued wearing the uniform, working with and instilling leadership in young people as a deputy commandant of the Virginia Tech Corps of Cadets for eight more years. His awards include the Medal of Honor, two Legion of Merit medals, the Bronze Star with Combat V, four Purple Heart awards, and numerous commendations. His first book was *Marine Rifleman: Forty-three Years in the Corps*, published by Potomac Books, Inc. (formerly Brassey's), in 2002.